D1518359

Central American Immigrants

Luis Martinez

Immigration to North America

Central American Immigrants

Luis Martinez

Senior Consulting Editor Stuart Anderson
former Associate Commissioner for Policy and Planning,
US. Citizenship and Immigration Services

Introduction by Marian L. Smith, Historian,
U.S. Citizenship and Immigration Services

Introduction by Peter A. Hammerschmidt,
former First Secretary, Permanent Mission of Canada to the United Nations

MC **MASON CREST**
PHILADELPHIA

Mason Crest
450 Parkway Drive, Suite D
Broomall, PA 19008
www.masoncrest.com

Printed and bound in the United States of America.

CPSIA Compliance Information: Batch #INA2016.
For further information, contact Mason Crest at 1-866-MCP-Book.

First printing
1 3 5 7 9 8 6 4 2

Library of Congress Cataloging-in-Publication Data

on file at the Library of Congress
ISBN: 978-1-4222-3686-4 (hc)
ISBN: 978-1-4222-8103-1 (ebook)

Immigration to North America series ISBN: 978-1-4222-3679-6

Table of Contents

KEY ICONS TO LOOK FOR:

 Words to Understand: These words with their easy-to-understand definitions will increase the reader's understanding of the text, while building vocabulary skills.

 Sidebars: This boxed material within the main text allows readers to build knowledge, gain insights, explore possibilities, and broaden their perspectives by weaving together additional information to provide realistic and holistic perspectives.

 Research Projects: Readers are pointed toward areas of further inquiry connected to each chapter. Suggestions are provided for projects that encourage deeper research and analysis.

 Text-Dependent Questions: These questions send the reader back to the text for more careful attention to the evidence presented there.

 Series Glossary of Key Terms: This back-of-the book glossary contains terminology used throughout this series. Words found here increase the reader's ability to read and comprehend higher-level books and articles in this field.

The Changing Face of the United States

Marian L. Smith, Historian
U.S. Citizenship and Immigration Services

Americans commonly assume that immigration today is very different than immigration of the past. The immigrants themselves appear to be unlike immigrants of earlier eras. Their language, their dress, their food, and their ways seem strange. At times people fear too many of these new immigrants will destroy the America they know. But has anything really changed? Do new immigrants have any different effect on America than old immigrants a century ago? Is the American fear of too much immigration a new development? Do immigrants really change America more than America changes the immigrants? The very subject of immigration raises many questions.

In the United States, immigration is more than a chapter in a history book. It is a continuous thread that links the present moment to the first settlers on North American shores. From the first colonists' arrival until today, immigrants have been met by Americans who both welcomed and feared them. Immigrant contributions were always welcome—on the farm, in the fields, and in the factories. Welcoming the poor, the persecuted, and the "huddled masses" became an American principle. Beginning with the original Pilgrims' flight from religious persecution in the 1600s, through the Irish migration to escape starvation in the 1800s, to the relocation of Central Americans seeking refuge from civil wars in the 1980s and 1990s, the United States has considered itself a haven for the destitute and the oppressed.

But there was also concern that immigrants would not adopt American ways, habits, or language. Too many immigrants might overwhelm America. If so, the dream of the Founding Fathers for United States government and society would be destroyed. For this reason, throughout American history some have argued that limiting or ending immigration is our patriotic duty. Benjamin Franklin feared there were so many German immigrants in Pennsylvania the Colonial Legislature would begin speaking German. "Progressive" leaders of the early 1900s feared that immigrants who could not read and understand the English language were not only exploited by "big business," but also served as the foundation for "machine politics" that undermined the U.S. Constitution. This theme continues today, usually voiced by those who bear no malice toward immigrants but who want to preserve American ideals.

Have immigrants changed? In colonial days, when most colonists were of English descent, they considered Germans, Swiss, and French immigrants as different. They were not "one of us" because they spoke a different language. Generations later, Americans of German or French descent viewed Polish, Italian, and Russian immigrants as strange. They were not "like us" because they had a different religion, or because they did not come from a tradition of constitutional government. Recently, Americans of Polish or Italian descent have seen Nicaraguan, Pakistani, or Vietnamese immigrants as too different to be included. It has long been said of American immigration that the latest ones to arrive usually want to close the door behind them.

It is important to remember that fear of individual immigrant groups seldom lasted, and always lessened. Benjamin Franklin's anxiety over German immigrants disappeared after those immigrants' sons and daughters helped the nation gain independence in the Revolutionary War. The Irish of the mid-1800s were among the most hated immigrants, but today we all wear green on St. Patrick's Day. While a century ago it was feared that Italian and other Catholic immigrants would vote as directed by the Pope, today that controversy is only a vague memory. Unfortunately, some ethnic groups continue their efforts to earn acceptance. The African

Americans' struggle continues, and some Asian Americans, whose families have been in America for generations, are the victims of current anti-immigrant sentiment.

Time changes both immigrants and America. Each wave of new immigrants, with their strange language and habits, eventually grows old and passes away. Their American-born children speak English. The immigrants' grandchildren are completely American. The strange foods of their ancestors—spaghetti, baklava, hummus, or tofu—become common in any American restaurant or grocery store. Much of what the immigrants brought to these shores is lost, principally their language. And what is gained becomes as American as St. Patrick's Day, Hanukkah, or Cinco de Mayo, and we forget that it was once something foreign.

Recent immigrants are all around us. They come from every corner of the earth to join in the American Dream. They will continue to help make the American Dream a reality, just as all the immigrants who came before them have done.

Welcome to the
United States
A Guide for New
Immigrants

UNITED STATES OF AMERICA   Department of Homeland Security

PERMANENT RESIDENT CARD

UNITED STATES OF AME

We recommend you use this enve
granted your new card.

The Changing Face of Canada

Peter A. Hammerschmidt
former First Secretary, Permanent Mission of Canada to the United Nations

Throughout Canada's history, immigration has shaped and defined the very character of Canadian society. The migration of peoples from every part of the world into Canada has profoundly changed the way we look, speak, eat, and live. Through close and distant relatives who left their lands in search of a better life, all Canadians have links to immigrant pasts. We are a nation built by and of immigrants.

Two parallel forces have shaped the history of Canadian immigration. The enormous diversity of Canada's immigrant population is the most obvious. In the beginning came the enterprising settlers of the "New World," the French and English colonists. Soon after came the Scottish, Irish, and Northern and Central European farmers of the 1700s and 1800s. As the country expanded westward during the mid-1800s, migrant workers began arriving from China, Japan, and other Asian countries. And the turbulent twentieth century brought an even greater variety of immigrants to Canada, from the Caribbean, Africa, India, and Southeast Asia.

So while English- and French-Canadians are the largest ethnic groups in the country today, neither group alone represents a majority of the population. A large and vibrant multicultural mix makes up the rest, particularly in Canada's major cities. Toronto, Vancouver, and Montreal alone are home to people from over 200 ethnic groups!

Less obvious but equally important in the evolution of Canadian immigration has been hope. The promise of a better life lured Europeans and

Americans seeking cheap (sometimes even free) farmland. Thousands of Scots and Irish arrived to escape grinding poverty and starvation. Others came for freedom, to escape religious and political persecution. Canada has long been a haven to the world's dispossessed and disenfranchised—Dutch and German farmers cast out for their religious beliefs, black slaves fleeing the United States, and political refugees of despotic regimes in Europe, Africa, Asia, and South America.

The two forces of diversity and hope, so central to Canada's past, also shaped the modern era of Canadian immigration. Following the Second World War, Canada drew heavily on these influences to forge trailblazing immigration initiatives.

The catalyst for change was the adoption of the Canadian Bill of Rights in 1960. Recognizing its growing diversity and Canadians' changing attitudes towards racism, the government passed a federal statute barring discrimination on the grounds of race, national origin, color, religion, or sex. Effectively rejecting the discriminatory elements in Canadian immigration policy, the Bill of Rights forced the introduction of a new policy in 1962. The focus of immigration abruptly switched from national origin to the individual's potential contribution to Canadian society. The door to Canada was now open to every corner of the world.

Welcoming those seeking new hopes in a new land has also been a feature of Canadian immigration in the modern era. The focus on economic immigration has increased along with Canada's steadily growing economy, but political immigration has also been encouraged. Since 1945, Canada has admitted tens of thousands of displaced persons, including Jewish Holocaust survivors, victims of Soviet crackdowns in Hungary and Czechoslovakia, and refugees from political upheaval in Uganda, Chile, and Vietnam.

Prior to 1978, however, these political refugees were admitted as an exception to normal immigration procedures. That year, Canada revamped its refugee policy with a new Immigration Act that explicitly affirmed Canada's commitment to the resettlement of refugees from oppression. Today, the admission of refugees remains a central part of

Canadian immigration law and regulations.

Amendments to economic and political immigration policy have continued, refining further the bold steps taken during the modern era. Together, these initiatives have turned Canada into one of the world's few truly multicultural states.

Unlike the process of assimilation into a "melting pot" of cultures, immigrants to Canada are more likely to retain their cultural identity, beliefs, and practices. This is the source of some of Canada's greatest strengths as a society. And as a truly multicultural nation, diversity is not seen as a threat to Canadian identity. Quite the contrary—diversity is Canadian identity.

1

THE PULL
OF EL NORTE

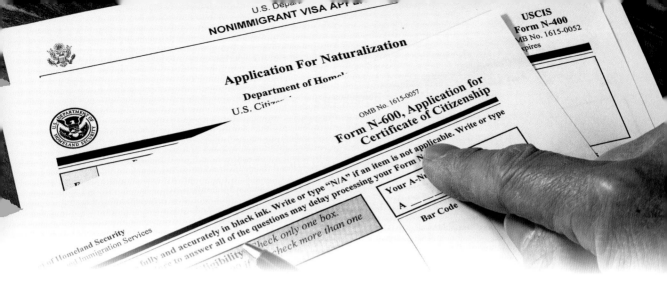

The face of America is changing. In the year 2010, according to the U.S. Census Bureau, about one in six people living in the United States—some 50.5 million individuals—claimed Hispanic ancestry. And each year tens of thousands of others leave their homelands to make the journey to El Norte in search of a better life.

More than half of all Latinos in the United States have roots in Mexico, which annually contributes more immigrants to its northern neighbor, by far, than any other country in the world. In recent years, however, immigrants from the seven nations of Central America—Belize, Costa Rica, El Salvador, Guatemala, Honduras, Nicaragua, and Panama—have also established vibrant, growing communities in the United States.

Between 2000 and 2010, more than 1.2 million people left Central America and settled legally in the United States or Canada (Canada welcomed nearly 100,000 of the total). And the trend continues. In 2015, according to the Center for Immigration Studies (CIS), three Central American countries—El Salvador, Guatemala, and Honduras—ranked among the top 20 source nations for legal immigrants to the United States. The combined immigrant population from these three countries to the U.S. has grown 234 percent since 1990.

◀ New U.S. citizen Aurelia Lopez holds her daughter and proudly displays her certificate of naturalization shortly after taking the oath of citizenship in Fort Lauderdale, Florida. More than 44,000 immigrants from Central America became U.S. citizens in 2013.

Legal immigration, however, is only part of the story. Millions of foreign-born people live in the United States (and, to a lesser extent, Canada) without proper documentation, and a significant proportion come from Central America. In fact, according to Department of Homeland Security (DHS) estimates for 2012, three Central American nations ranked among the top 10 source countries for undocumented immigrants living in the United States. Specifically, the overall rankings and estimated number of undocumented immigrants were: El Salvador, second (690,000); Guatemala, third (560,000); and Honduras, fourth (360,000).

Diverse Peoples and Cultures

Ethnically and culturally, Central American immigrants represent a diverse group. There are significant differences among Salvadorans, Guatemalans, Hondurans, Nicaraguans, Panamanians, Costa Ricans, and Belizeans, and the people of each country take great pride in their unique heritage. Most Central Americans speak Spanish, but the official language of Belize is English, which is also widely used on the Atlantic coast of Nicaragua. In addition, various Amerindian tongues are spoken throughout Central America; in Guatemala alone there are about two dozen such languages. The Central Americans who immigrate to the United States and Canada may be white or black, Amerindian or mestizo (of mixed European and Native American ancestry). Some are doctors, lawyers, and business executives, but many more come from impoverished backgrounds.

While the United States, at different times in its history, sought to close its doors to various immigrant groups, Central

 Words to Understand in This Chapter

Amerindian—a person descended from Native Americans.

civil war—a war between people of the same nation.

refugee—a person who flees a country because of the threat of violence, war, or persecution.

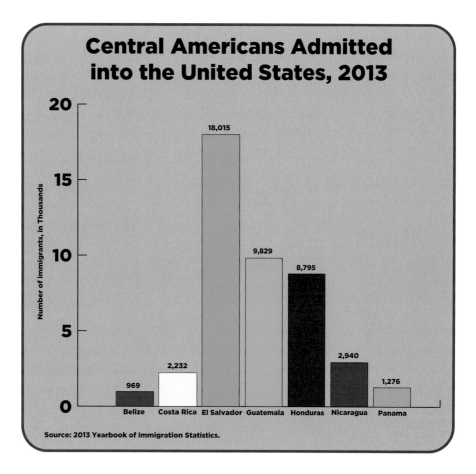

Central Americans Admitted into the United States, 2013

Number of Immigrants, in Thousands

- Belize: 969
- Costa Rica: 2,232
- El Salvador: 18,015
- Guatemala: 9,829
- Honduras: 8,795
- Nicaragua: 2,940
- Panama: 1,276

Source: 2013 Yearbook of Immigration Statistics.

Americans never specifically faced restrictions the way, for example, immigrants from China or Japan did. Nevertheless, relatively few Central Americans settled in the United States or Canada until the last decades of the 20th century. But when political violence and full-blown civil wars engulfed much of the region, tens of thousands of people fled north. More than 200,000 Guatemalans, for example, immigrated to the United States and Canada during their country's 36-year-long civil war, which finally ended in 1996. And as many as half a million Salvadorans, the majority undocumented, sought refuge in North America during the 1980s, when rebels fought El Salvador's government, and paramilitary "death squads" kidnapped and murdered thousands of civilians.

Today the countries of Central America are at peace with their neighbors, but social problems such as widespread poverty and drug-related corruption and violence persist. Economic development in the region has been stifled by the years of war, corrupt governments, and even natural disasters such as 1998's Hurricane Mitch. So each year, tens of thousands of Central Americans continue to make the often-arduous journey to the United States or Canada. Many are so desperate to escape the bleak prospects in their homeland that they are willing to risk their lives crossing the Mexico-U.S. border, walking across searing deserts or braving a dangerous swim across the Rio Grande.

Settling In

When they arrive in the United States or Canada, these immigrants flock to friendly communities from coast to coast. Today eclectic neighborhoods such as Los Angeles's Pico-Union and Miami's Sweetwater are defined by the Central American immigrants who dwell there. But Central Americans also live in cities and small towns just about everywhere in between. These immigrants enrich Hispanic culture in the United States, where Latinos are now the largest minority group.

As they settle in, Central American immigrants—much like immigrants from all over the world—gradually begin to assimilate. The process is complicated. On the one hand, immigrants typically want to embrace the values and opportunities their new country has to offer. On the other, they frequently cling to traditions and customs from home. In many cases, immigrants try to keep one foot in their adopted country, the other planted in the country of their birth. Central American immigrants may learn to speak English, but many continue to speak Spanish at home. They may join the festivities on the Fourth of July, but they also celebrate the *fiestas patronales* of their homelands. They may dine on meatloaf, but they still find a plate of rice and beans or tamales more delicious. They may adopt a favorite baseball team, but they never stop obsessing about *fútbol* (soccer).

Many Central American immigrants living and working in North America send money home to impoverished loved ones. Annually, these remittances total billions of dollars, and they sustain not only individual families but also entire towns. To a certain extent, even the national economies of some of the Central American countries now depend on the flow of immigrant money.

But while many Central Americans are lured north by visions of prosperity—and while they often can, in fact, make more money in the United States or Canada than they could in their homeland—the transition to life in North America is rarely smooth. Many of the immigrants, lacking a college education or extensive job skills, have no options except low-wage work. Some encounter discrimination in the workplace. Many struggle to support their families.

As with people from all over the world, many Central Americans move to the United States or Canada so that their children might have a better life. Educational opportunities are a major draw. But many financially strapped public schools are overwhelmed by the special needs of students who arrive in their classrooms speaking little or no English.

As much as they love and cherish their native countries, Central Americans continue to travel to *El Norte*. They know about the struggles and hardships. They also know the success stories—of Central American immigrant children who have grown up to be astronauts, judges, or authors. A couple of decades ago they came for peace and liberty. Today they want to give their children the chance to be anything they want to be.

 # Text-Dependent Questions

1. What are the seven nations of Central America?
2. What is the term for a person of mixed European and Native American ancestry?

 # Research Project

Using a library of the Internet, investigate one of Central America's seven nations. Present the following basic information: Population; Capital city; Other major cities. Then write three to four paragraphs on any aspects of the capital city that you found especially interesting.

2 CENTRAL AMERICA: THE COST OF WAR AND POVERTY

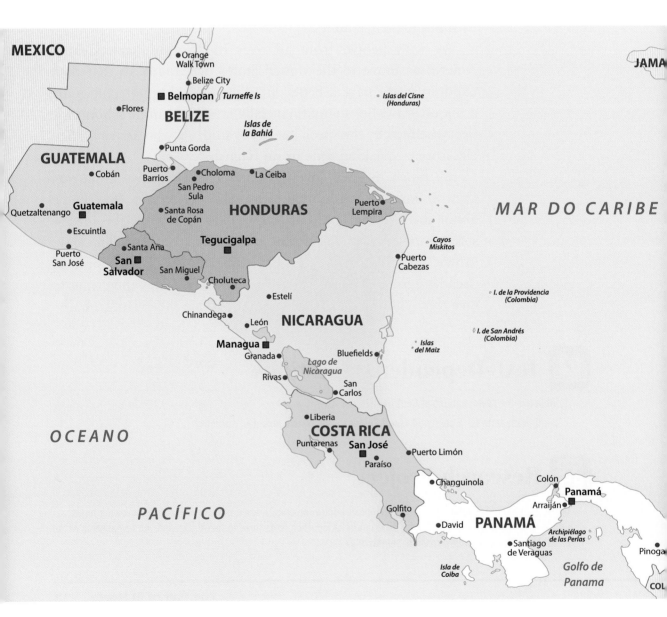

MEXICO

● Orange Walk Town

● Belize City

■ **Belmopan** *Turneffe Is*

● Flores

BELIZE

● Punta Gorda

Islas del Cisne (Honduras)

Islas de la Bahiá

GUATEMALA

● Cobán

Puerto Barrios ●

● Choloma   ● La Ceiba

San Pedro Sula ●

● Santa Rosa de Copán

HONDURAS

Puerto Lempira ●

Guatemala ■

Quetzaltenango ●

MAR DO CARIBE

● Escuintla

Puerto San José ●

● Santa Ana

San ■ **Salvador**

Tegucigalpa ●

San Miguel ●

● Choluteca

● Puerto Cabezas

Cayos Miskitos

● Estelí

I. de la Providencia (Colombia)

Chinandega ●

● León

NICARAGUA

◊ *I. de San Andrés (Colombia)*

OCEANO

Managua ■

Granada ●

Lago de Nicaragua

Bluefields ●

● *Islas del Maiz*

Rivas ●

San Carlos ●

● Liberia

COSTA RICA

Puntarenas ●

San José ■

● Puerto Limón

Paraíso ●

Colón ●

Panamá ■

PACÍFICO

● Changuinola

Golfito ●

Arraiján ●

● David

PANAMÁ

Archipiélago de las Perlas

Pinoga

● Santiago de Veraguas

Isla de Coiba

Golfo de Panama

COL

JAMA

The Central American isthmus stretches some 1,700 miles from Mexico to Colombia. The land bridge is made up of rolling hills and mountains, verdant rain forests, and sandy beaches. To the outsider, the region's natural splendor might make it seem like a paradise, and most Central Americans love their country of birth. But every year, tens of thousands of emigrants leave for the United States or Canada.

The difficult decision to move to a new country may be motivated by many factors, but historically several stand out as particularly important. War or high levels of political violence typically spur emigration because they make people fear for their safety, perhaps the most basic of all motivations to leave one's home. The desire for freedom from political repression or ethnic or religious persecution is another powerful motivator. Economic conditions also play a key role. Where poverty is widespread and job and educational opportunities are slim, people are more inclined to consider leaving their homeland. And it is often the more courageous or entrepreneurial who are willing to take a chance on life in a new land.

All of these factors have been present in modern Central America (though the experiences of the seven nations in the region differ significantly). Civil wars have torn apart Central

◀ Chronic poverty, civil wars, and most recently drug-related violence and political corruption have spurred hundreds of thousands of Central Americans to make the long journey north to the United States and Canada.

American societies and claimed hundreds of thousands of lives. Until fairly recently, repressive, authoritarian governments were the rule. And poverty has been—and continues to be—a major problem; most nations in the region suffer from a starkly unequal distribution of income, with a tiny elite controlling the lion's share of the wealth, and the majority of the populace living in difficult conditions.

El Salvador: The Ravages of War

Nestled between Guatemala and Honduras and bounded on the west by the Pacific Ocean, El Salvador is Central America's smallest nation by area, but its third largest by population. A rugged land, it is covered by two mountain ranges containing many volcanic peaks. The soil and the climate are ideal for the cultivation of coffee, which since the mid-1800s has been El Salvador's most important cash crop.

Over time land, wealth, and political influence in El Salvador were increasingly concentrated in the hands of a few families who controlled the country's coffee industry. By the 20th century, coffee exports accounted for about 95 percent of El Salvador's income, yet just 2 percent of the population controlled all that wealth. The sprawling plantations of the coffee growers depended on a pool of cheap labor, and because so many campesinos (rural dwellers) were landless, the growers could dictate wages and working conditions, which were dismal. An uprising among the rural poor during the early 1930s was

 Words to Understand in This Chapter

emigrant—a person who moves away from a country.

isthmus—a narrow strip of land connecting two larger landmasses.

left-wing—having a radical or very liberal political affiliation or outlook.

right-wing—having a very conservative or reactionary political affiliation or outlook.

brutally crushed as El Salvador's army and National Guard (an organization responsible for internal security and police functions, primarily in rural areas), in combination with paramilitary groups in the service of local landowners, killed some 10,000 peasants. For the next half-century the military kept a firm grip on the reins of government. Presidential elections were routinely rigged.

Between 1960 and the mid-1970s, the pace of rural landlessness accelerated. In the absence of land reform, several small guerrilla groups, which sought to overthrow the government by force, were established. In response, armed pro-government factions targeted not simply revolutionary leaders but also ordinary people with liberal political views. Although a group of reform-minded military officers staged a coup in October 1979, significant improvements in El Salvador's political and social situation failed to materialize.

In 1980 Oscar Romero, the Catholic archbishop of San Salvador, was assassinated, presumably by supporters of the military government. Romero had called for El Salvador's leaders to stop repressing their citizens. The murder of the popular archbishop spurred a large demonstration, which police broke up by firing into the crowd. By the end of the year, the unrest had exploded into a full-scale civil war.

The main antigovernment force, the Farabundo Martí National Liberation Front—known by the Spanish acronym FMLN—received support from Cuba and, at least indirectly, the Soviet Union. Fearing that an FMLN victory would bring a Communist regime to power, the United States—particularly during the administration of President Ronald Reagan (1981–89)—funneled more than a billion dollars in military and economic aid to the Salvadoran government. Critics have charged that U.S. support for the Salvadoran regime—as well as American involvement in conflicts in Guatemala and Nicaragua—worsened conditions in Central America during the 1980s. "The origins and spiraling intensity of those wars were a direct result of military and economic intervention by our own

Rebels of the FMLN (Frente Farabundo Marti para la Liberacion Nacional) celebrate a cease-fire in the Salvadoran civil war, 1992. Their vehicle is accompanied by U.N. peacekeeping troops.

government," writes Juan Gonzalez in *Harvest of Empire: A History of Latinos in America*.

In El Salvador, the civil war raged for 12 years. Although government forces fought FMLN rebels in the mountains and jungles, the vast majority of victims in that conflict—perhaps as many as 65,000 of the estimated 75,000 killed—were civilians. Army and National Guard units are reported to have massacred thousands of villagers in an effort to quash support for the rebels. Right-wing "death squads"—paramilitary groups that operated with at least the tacit approval of the armed forces and government—kidnapped, tortured, and murdered those suspected of harboring sympathies for the FMLN. But the army, National Guard, and paramilitaries had no monopoly on human rights abuses. When the FMLN occupied rural towns or villages, for example, it routinely executed mayors, other officials, and suspected supporters of the government. A 1993 United Nations report found substantial human rights abuses on all sides of the civil war, though most of the blame was assigned to El Salvador's armed forces and death squads.

In the face of the horrific violence, an estimated one million Salvadorans fled their country. Many headed for North America.

In 1990 the rebels and the Salvadoran government agreed to begin United Nations–mediated negotiations to end the conflict. In early 1992 peace accords were signed, and a cease-fire went into effect. As part of the peace treaty, military reforms were enacted, a national police force was organized, some land was redistributed to campesinos, and the FMLN became a legitimate political party. Beginning in 1994, free elections were held for El Salvador's presidency and parliament. By the election of 2003, the FMLN controlled more seats in parliament than any other political party.

In 1999, Francisco Flores was elected president. He was backed by the conservative Nationalist Republican Alliance (ARENA). Flores was president until 2004. His term ended in scandal when he was found to have diverted over $15 million dollars from Taiwan. The money was intended to help victims of the 2001 earthquake that struck El Salvador, but Flores instead kept a third for himself and gave the remainder to ARENA. The earthquakes killed 2,000 people and destroyed or damaged one of every four homes. Flores died in 2016, while he was still under house arrest.

ARENA candidate Tony Saca was elected president in 2004, followed in 2009 by Mauricio Funes of the FMLN party. Funes, a leftist, was a former Marxist rebel. He, in turn, was followed by Salvador Sanchez Ceren, who took office in 2014. He, too is affiliated with the FMLN party.

El Salvador continues to confront massive economic and social problems. The civil war devastated the country's infrastructure, and El Salvador's limited economic resources have hampered rebuilding efforts. To add to the misery of the 2001 earthquakes, the Ilamatepec (or Santa Ana) Volcano erupted in 2005, forcing thousands from their homes. And a few days after that, Tropical Storm Stan killed scores of people.

In addition to natural disasters, El Salvador has had to contend with a growing drug problem. In 2011, the United States added El Salvador to a list of countries which it considers to be heavily involved in drug production and/or trafficking.

Because the country continues to depend heavily on coffee exports, its economy is hit hard by any downturn in international coffee prices. And perhaps most troublingly, inequality in the distribution of wealth—one of the primary causes of the civil war—continues. In 2013 El Salvador's richest 20 percent enjoyed 50 percent of the country's income; by contrast, the share of the poorest 20 percent was just 5.5 percent. However, by some measures life in El Salvador is improving. In 2001, almost half of El Salvador's population lived in poverty. In 2013, that proportion had dropped to one-third of El Salvador's 6.1 million people living in poverty. In 2001, nearly 30 out of every 1,000 babies born died before their first birthday. In 2015, that number was 14, or an improvement of more than 50 percent. Nearly 85 percent of adults in the country are literate, which is up from 80 percent in 2001.

Even so, largely because of the persistent economic troubles, significant numbers of Salvadorans continue to immigrate to the United States and Canada.

Guatemala: Conflict and Poverty

North and west of El Salvador lies Guatemala, which also shares borders with Honduras and Belize to the east and Mexico to the north. Guatemala is far and away Central America's most populous country: its 2016 population of about 16 million was nearly double that of the region's next largest nation, Honduras.

Guatemala also boasts an exceedingly rich history. It was a center of one of the most advanced civilizations in the New World, the Maya. Mayan culture, which reached its peak in the period A.D. 250–900, produced magnificent monumental buildings, beautiful works of art, and advanced mathematical and astronomical knowledge. The Mayan city of Tikal, in present-day northern Guatemala, is justly celebrated as one of the world's most magnificent and important archaeological sites.

Many Guatemalans today are proud of, and hold on to, their Mayan heritage. More than 4 in 10 Guatemalans are fully or predominantly Amerindian in ancestry and have not assimilated into the mainstream culture. Some 40 percent of the country's people speak a Native American language, nearly two dozen of which are officially recognized. This is in marked contrast to other countries of the region, such as Nicaragua, where Spanish conquest and colonization beginning in the 1500s all but wiped out indigenous culture.

But for all its past glory, Guatemala's recent history has been very troubled. After becoming an independent republic in 1839, the country was ruled by a series of dictators until a revolution in 1944 brought free elections for the presidency. Juan José

 The Peacemakers

Central America in the latter half of the 20th century was wracked by political violence and warfare. But two of the region's inhabitants won the world's most prestigious peace award for their work in ending conflicts and promoting justice.

Oscar Arias Sánchez, elected president of Costa Rica in 1986, made resolution of Central America's long-standing conflicts one of his top priorities. Only months after taking office, he met with the presidents of Guatemala, El Salvador, Nicaragua, and Honduras in an effort to move forward peace discussions. That meeting ended without an agreement, but early the following year, Arias again brought the Central American leaders together and submitted a plan he had worked out. His framework for regional peace led to an accord signed by the Central American presidents in August of 1987. Arias was awarded the Nobel Peace Prize for his efforts.

Rigoberta Menchú Tum, a Maya Indian from the highlands of Guatemala, experienced first-hand the brutality of the region's conflicts. Guatemalan security forces killed her father and later tortured and killed her mother and brother. Menchú became a human rights activist and an advocate for her country's Indian peoples. Forced to flee to Mexico, she continued to work tirelessly to raise awareness of the plight of Guatemala's indigenous population. Her autobiography, translated into English as *I, Rigoberta Menchú: An Indian Woman in Guatemala,* presented a stark and compelling picture. In 1992 the Nobel Committee awarded Menchú the Peace Prize for her commitment to the cause of justice and human rights.

Arévalo, an intellectual and former university professor, won that first election in a landslide. Arévalo promoted labor reform and social programs, such as a literacy campaign. While some of his administration's socialist rhetoric may have alarmed Guatemala's landed upper class—whose interests the country's former rulers had consistently served—Guatemalan society did not radically change during Arévalo's presidency.

But his successor, Jacobo Arbenz Guzmán, was determined to enact major social and economic reforms. Elected president in 1950, Arbenz—a leftist whose wife was an avowed Communist—quickly ran afoul of the U.S. government. American officials feared that Guatemala's president might provide the Soviet Union with an opportunity to gain a foothold in Latin America—something they were determined to prevent. Concerns were raised by Arbenz's land-reform program, which included the transfer to Guatemalan ownership of some property held by foreign companies. The United Fruit Company, an American-owned firm that produced bananas, was the most prominent company targeted. At the time, United Fruit was Guatemala's single largest landholder and employer; it also controlled the country's rail system.

In 1954 a coup sponsored by the U.S. Central Intelligence Agency forced Arbenz from office. The coup leader, a retired colonel named Carlos Castillo Armas, became Guatemala's president.

What followed was a succession of repressive military rulers and decades of nightmarish violence. In the early 1960s, after the assassination of Castillo Armas and a pair of unsuccessful coup attempts, rebel groups formed to topple Guatemala's government through a guerrilla war. The fighting raged for more than 35 years. The army, with aid from the United States, waged a brutal campaign against the guerrillas in the Guatemalan countryside. The rebels carried out counterstrikes and assassinations. Death squads murdered countless civilians.

Guatemala's Maya Indians, who lived in the countryside where the guerrillas operated, were frequently caught in the mid-

United Nations Secretary-General Kofi Annan (right) meets with Rigoberta Menchu of Guatemala, who received the 1992 Nobel Peace Prize for her human rights work, particularly on behalf of indigenous peoples.

dle. But because they were thought to sympathize with the rebels, the Mayans were also directly targeted. The slaughter was particularly terrible in the early 1980s, during the regime of General Efraín Rios Montt. The general infamously told a group of Mayans, "If you are with us, we'll feed you. If not, we'll kill you." According to later reports by the United Nations, human rights groups, and a Guatemalan "truth commission," hundreds of villages were completely destroyed and their inhabitants— men, women, and children—murdered.

In the 1980s, various guerrilla factions united to form the Guatemalan National Revolutionary Unity (known by its Spanish acronym, URNG). But the URNG failed to achieve significant military successes. Meanwhile, in 1985 and again in 1991, Guatemalans chose their president in national elections, the first peaceful and democratic transfer of power the country had witnessed since 1950. In 1991 peace talks between the government and the URNG began, but the negotiations soon bogged down.

Finally, in the spring of 1996, the URNG declared a cease-fire and the government responded by suspending its military operations. In December of that year, with Alvaro Arzu serving as president, the two sides finally hammered out a peace treaty.

All told, the conflict in Guatemala—Central America's longest-running civil war—claimed the lives of as many as 200,000 people, according to a report by the country's Historical Clarification Commission. The majority were civilians and Mayan Indians. In addition, an estimated one million Guatemalans fled their homes.

The years since 1996 have been difficult. Although a measure of political stability has returned, Guatemala is still rebuilding after the decades of violence. In 2004, a United Nations commission found that Guatemala was still plagued by crime, injustice, and human rights violations. In 2007, Amnesty International asked Guatemala's government to address the country's fast-rising murder rate. Several political candidates were murdered in the run-up to elections. In recent years, some of Guatemala's presidents have been accused of crimes that include murder and embezzlement.

In 2009, Guatemalans faced severe food shortages The nation's underdeveloped economy relies heavily on agricultural exports, particularly coffee, sugar, and bananas. A drop in the prices

The American businessman and financier Cornelius Vanderbilt established a transportation route across Nicaragua in 1850. During much of the succeeding century and a half, U.S. involvement in Nicaragua—both commercial and military—would prove controversial.

of these commodities, especially coffee, can be a major blow.

An estimated 8 million Guatemalans—just over half of the nation's population—live in poverty. The infant mortality rate stands at 24 deaths per 1,000 births. Though high, this represents an enormous improvement over the country's 2001 rate of more than 44 infant deaths per 1,000 births, which at the time was the highest rate in Central America. In 2015, 76 percent of Guatemalan adults were able to read and write.

Nicaragua: The Legacy of War

As with El Salvador and Guatemala, civil strife has left its mark on Nicaragua. Once fairly prosperous, the country—which is situated between Honduras to the north and Costa Rica to the south—had by the beginning of the 21st century become Central America's most impoverished nation, and one of the poorest in the entire Western Hemisphere.

The United States has played a significant role in the modern history of Nicaragua, which gained complete independence in 1838. In 1850, during the California gold rush, the American businessman Cornelius Vanderbilt paid the Nicaraguan government $10,000 for the right to set up a transportation route across the Central American country. Vanderbilt's route—which made use of steamships on the San Juan River and Lake Nicaragua, and stagecoaches on a 12-mile road his company constructed in western Nicaragua—shortened the journey from New York to San Francisco. As a result, the American businessman made a handsome profit—and garnered considerable influence in Nicaragua. In 1855, however, an adventurer from Tennessee named William Walker landed on Nicaragua's Pacific coast with 57 armed men and, by exploiting a factional conflict between liberals and conservatives, proceeded to take over the country. Walker made himself president, but his tenure was brief. After he revoked Vanderbilt's transit rights across Nicaragua, Vanderbilt organized a large armed force to oust the Tennessean, which was accomplished by 1857.

In the latter part of the 19th century, as the United States considered building a canal across Central America, it was widely assumed that the route would be through Nicaragua. For various reasons, however, Panama was eventually chosen. José Santos Zelaya, a tyrant who ruled Nicaragua from 1894 until 1909, threatened to sell the rights to build a canal through his country to Japan or another potential U.S. rival. Eventually the United States paid Nicaragua $3 million to ensure that did not happen.

Under pressure from the U.S. government, Zelaya was forced from power in 1909. Nicaragua was heavily in debt, and after a pro-American regime came to power, the United States arranged loans for the struggling country. But troubles continued. By 1912, with Nicaragua on the verge of a revolution, President William Howard Taft dispatched a contingent of U.S. Marines. With the exception of a brief period beginning in August 1925, the marines would maintain a continuous presence in Nicaragua until 1933.

Resentment of the American occupation ran high. A guerrilla leader, Augusto Sandino, harassed the marines relentlessly for years, in the process winning almost mythic status among the Nicaraguan people.

After the Americans departed Nicaragua in 1933, order was maintained by the National Guard, a force that the marines had created. The leader of the National Guard, Anastasio Somoza García, soon maneuvered himself into the presidency—and established a political dynasty that would last from 1936 until 1979.

Upon gaining the presidency, Somoza—known widely as "Tacho"—quickly assumed the role of dictator. He ruthlessly suppressed dissent. He used his power to enrich himself and his family, amassing a fortune in the tens of millions of dollars. He also maintained good relations with the United States, in large part because of his staunch anticommunism. After Tacho's assassination in 1956, his sons—first Luis and then Anastasio—would follow the same pattern of intimidating and repressing their people, misappropriating public funds, and successfully cultivating the support of the United States.

Yet during the long, tyrannical rule of the Somoza family, Nicaragua did experience periods of economic progress. The 1960s, in particular, were a boom time, with expanded investment, factory construction, and cotton production. But while the upper and middle classes prospered, Nicaragua's peasants saw few of the benefits of this economic growth.

Luis Somoza made some effort to govern less repressively than had his father—or at least to appear to do so. Soon after his younger brother Anastasio took over in 1967, however, Nicaraguans experienced a brutal political crackdown, along with unrestrained corruption. Anastasio Somoza used the National Guard (which he headed) to intimidate—and, if necessary, torture and kill—critics and opponents. But Somoza's tactics only increased opposition to his regime, which in turn led to even more brutality on the part of the dictator.

A devastating earthquake struck the Nicaraguan capital of Managua in 1972, killing 10,000 and leaving another 50,000 homeless. The disaster strained Nicaragua's economy, which had already begun to slump, and Nicaraguans at all levels of society were enraged when it was discovered that Somoza and the National Guard were stealing international aid intended for the earthquake victims. Somoza declared martial law to stifle the opposition.

In 1974 members of the Sandinista National Liberation Front, a Marxist guerrilla group that had been founded in the early 1960s, seized a home where a handful of government officials, including members of the Somoza family, were staying. The rebel group—known by the Spanish acronym FSLN—forced the Nicaraguan government to pay a million-dollar ransom, to release more than a dozen Sandinista prisoners, and to read a statement on the radio. The incident marked a turning point in the effort to oust the Somoza regime. Even though the government launched a brutal campaign to stamp out the FSLN and its supporters, the revolution gained momentum.

In 1978, in the face of widespread human rights abuses per-

A display of weapons surrendered to the soldiers of the United Nations Observer Group in Central America (ONUCA) by the Nicaraguan resistance forces as part of the overall peace process in Central America, 1990.

petrated by the Nicaraguan government and National Guard, the U.S. administration of President Jimmy Carter cut off aid to the Somoza regime. By the following year, the regime's position had grown perilous. A variety of opposition groups united, and on the battlefield the rebels gained the upper hand. On July 17, 1979, Anastasio Somoza resigned. Two days later, the rebels entered Managua and assumed power. The revolution had left some 50,000 Nicaraguans dead, and another 150,000 had fled the country.

Nicaragua's woes were not over, however. The new government was headed by a five-member junta representing all the major opposition groups, but gradually the Sandinistas, led by Daniel Ortega Saavedra, gained control. The Sandinista leadership, which was decidedly Marxist in orientation, turned to Cuba and the Soviet Union for aid—and in the process drew the ire of U.S. president Ronald Reagan. In 1981, the year the staunchly anticommunist Reagan took office, his administration—accusing the Sandinistas of fomenting revolution in El Salvador—authorized $119 million to fund rebels seeking to overthrow the Nicaraguan government. Many of the rebels—known as the contras, from the Spanish word *contrarevolucionario* ("counterrevolutionary")—were former members of Somoza's notorious National Guard. From their bases in neighboring Honduras, they crossed into Nicaragua and carried out hit-and-run raids.

Although the Sandinista government had an ambitious economic and social agenda, much of the country's limited resources had to be allocated to fighting the contras, and the government severely curtailed free speech and other civil liberties. During Ortega's rule, the Sandinistas were accused of many human rights abuses, including political arrests, executions, and land confiscations. Many middle-class professionals and other Nicaraguans fled to the United States, where they were welcomed as political refugees.

As the war dragged on, members of the United States Congress began to grow increasingly skeptical of the Reagan administration's Nicaragua policy. U.S. forces had mined a Nicaraguan harbor in violation of international law, and the contras' human rights record was said to be abysmal. In 1985 Congress voted to prohibit funding for the contras. The administration's efforts to skirt the congressional ban resulted in a major scandal known as Iran-contra.

By the late 1980s, both sides in the Nicaraguan conflict had good reasons to negotiate. The contras had little hope of winning an outright military victory, and American support for their cause had waned. The Sandinistas faced an economy devastated by nearly a decade of civil war following right on the heels of the long struggle to oust Anastasio Somoza. In 1988 the two sides agreed to a cease-fire (although peace would not be fully achieved for two more years), and national elections were scheduled for 1990.

In those elections, Violeta Chamorro, the candidate of a coalition of opposition parties, defeated FSLN head Daniel Ortega to gain the presidency. The Sandinistas were again defeated in the democratic elections of 1996 and 2001.

Although Nicaragua's government has attempted new economic and political reforms, huge problems remain. The country's economy is still recovering from the long years of conflict. A banking crisis in the early 2000s also hurt, and its effects have lingered. In 2002, former president Arnoldo Aleman was charged with money laundering and embezzlement while in office. He was convicted and sentenced to 20 years in prison, although he was later moved to house arrest.

Nicaragua's financial woes were addressed by the rest of the world in 2004. That year, the World Bank excused 80 percent of the country's debt to them, and a few months later Russia agreed to write off the billions of dollars that Nicaragua owed them from the Soviet era. The people of Nicaragua did not feel the relief, however, and in 2005 a series of street protests against the rising costs of living and fuel turned violent. In 2006, former president Daniel Ortega was re-elected. Ortega was elected again in 2011 in a landslide, despite information from the organization

Daniel Ortega was leader of the Sandinista National Liberation Front, which held power in Nicaragua between 1979 and 1990. Ortega was elected as Nicaragua's president in 2006 and has served in that position since then.

Wikileaks that indicated that the Ortega government was financed by the drug trade.

In 2015 it was estimated that nearly half of Nicaragua's 6 million residents lived in poverty. Inequality in the distribution of wealth is severe: the poorest 20 percent earn just 5 percent of the income, while the richest 20 percent earn 50 percent.

Honduras: A Storm's Devastation

Honduras, which borders Guatemala, El Salvador, and Nicaragua, had the good fortune to avoid the bloody civil conflicts that devastated its neighbors during the 1980s. But over the course of its history, Central America's second most populous nation has been something less than a model of stability. In fact, since declaring independence from Spain in 1821, Honduras has been torn by more than 300 revolts, wars, and coups.

The Honduran economy has long depended on the cultivation of bananas and coffee. By the second decade of the 20th century, bananas accounted for about two-thirds of the country's total exports, and three U.S. companies—United Fruit, Standard Fruit, and Cuyamel Fruit—controlled the lion's share of the business. Although these companies periodically meddled in Honduran politics, they also constructed schools and health-care clinics for the families of their workers. Still, conditions for most Hondurans remained quite poor, and by 1960 a small leftist movement had begun to form.

In 1963 an army colonel moved to head off any possible Communist-inspired disorder, wresting control of the government from an elected president and ushering in several decades of military control. But economic growth throughout the rest of the decade was impressive—until a war with neighboring El Salvador broke out in 1969. Tensions between the two countries had long been building over the demarcation of their border and over the presence of tens of thousands of Salvadoran immigrants in Honduras. But because what ignited the fighting was a World Cup qualifying tournament between the two countries, it became known as the Soccer War. On July 14, El Salvador bombed and invaded Honduras, which fought back with air strikes directed at its western neighbor. The Soccer War lasted less than a week, but it claimed the lives of as many as 3,000, about two-thirds of them Hondurans. Moreover, the economic disruption was severe and lasted for many years.

In 1982 the Honduran military finally yielded power to a democratically elected civilian government. Still, political repression persisted, and military and police death squads operated in Honduras throughout the 1980s (although their atrocities were not nearly as extensive as those committed by their counterparts in Guatemala or El Salvador). The victims of Honduran death squads during the 1980s—primarily left-wing political activists—are believed to number about 190.

Despite the human rights abuses, Honduras in the 1980s was a major recipient of U.S. aid, and a staunch American ally. Washington viewed Honduran bases as crucial in the contras' war against the Sandinista government of Nicaragua.

According to World Bank estimates, in 2013 nearly 65 percent of all Hondurans lived below the poverty line. Some of Honduras's economic troubles can be attributed to Hurricane Mitch, which slammed into the region in October 1998. Mitch hit Honduras harder than any other Central American country. The storm's heavy rains proved particularly destructive, causing floods and mudslides that wiped out entire villages, swept away a large part of the Honduran highway system, and devastated the country's banana plantations. The death toll reached 5,600, a million Hondurans were left homeless, and economic damages totaled over $1 billion. Despite large-scale international aid, Honduras has still not recovered fully. Due to shortages of jobs, a major source of income for many families in Honduras is remittances, the money sent home by relatives who have immigrated to the U.S.

Today, half of all Hondurans are under the age of 19. There is an epidemic of crime and violence in the nation, much of it conducted by "maras," or youth gangs. It is estimated that tens of thousands of young people belong to the maras, and they use violence and threats of violence to control poorer areas of the country.

In 2009, then-president Manuel Zelaya was deposed in a coup; he remained in exile until 2011. That same year, the U.S. Peace Corps recalled all its Honduran volunteers due to rising violence. Dozens of journalists have been killed in targeted attacks, and in 2012 a series of street protests called attention to these killings. That same year, two of Honduras's main street gangs agreed to a truce. In 2014, Juan Orlando Hernandez became president of Honduras.

In response to the continued wave of immigrants coming to the U.S. to escape violence and poverty, the U.S. has increased its aid to Honduras. The U.S. also earmarked millions to combat gangs and help repatriate Hondurans who have been deported from the United States. Currently, more than a half-million Hondurans are dealing with the devastation caused by a severe drought.

Panama: Land of the Canal

Panama, a narrow country bordered on the north by Costa Rica and on the south by Colombia, links North and South America. More important, thanks to the famous canal that cuts through the center of the country between Colón on the Caribbean and Balboa on the Gulf of Panama, it also links the Atlantic and Pacific Oceans.

The centuries-old dream of creating a waterway through Central America—thereby enabling ships to cross from the Atlantic to the Pacific without having to make the long and arduous voyage around the tip of South America—has shaped the history of Panama. Between 1879 and 1889 a French company tried unsuccessfully to build a canal across Panama, which at the time belonged to Colombia. Around the turn of the century, the United States planned a similar undertaking. But

Several freighters, assisted by tugboats, are entering the Panama Canal at Gatun Locks on the Atlantic side. These container ships are fully loaded with cargo heading west towards the Pacific.

American officials grew disenchanted with the course of negotiations with Colombia, so they encouraged a Panamanian revolt in 1903 and then prevented Colombian troops from moving against the insurrection. In this manner Panama gained its independence from Colombia and promptly ceded to the United States—in exchange for $10 million—a 10-mile-wide swath of land through which the canal would be built.

Between 1904 and 1914, the U.S. Army Corps of Engineers, using a labor force largely from the Caribbean, constructed the Panama Canal. One of the great engineering feats of the 20th century, the 50-mile-long waterway used a system of huge locks to raise ships the 85 feet from the Atlantic or Pacific coast to Lake Gatun. After sailing across the lake, a ship would then be lowered by locks to the opposite coast.

The United States maintained control of the Canal Zone and operated the Canal, each year collecting millions of dollars in tolls from the ships making the crossing. Panama received an annual rental fee. Panama also benefited from thousands of Canal jobs, along with the economic activity American Canal employees generated. Largely because of this, Panamanians enjoyed a higher standard of living than most Central Americans.

Panama's political culture was also less turbulent than that of most of the Central American countries. But by the middle of the 20th century, outbreaks of anti-Americanism occurred with some frequency. In 1964 violent demonstrations sparked by the removal of the Panamanian flag from a Canal Zone high school lasted for several days and claimed the lives of four American soldiers and 23 Panamanians.

In 1968 General Omar Torrijos ousted Panama's democratically elected president in a coup. Torrijos quickly dissolved the Panamanian legislature, banned political parties, and imposed strict censorship of the press. Yet under his regime economic growth was significant (the banking industry in particular took off) and social welfare became a priority. In addition, Torrijos pursued a policy that made him quite popular with Panama-

U.S. president Jimmy Carter and Panamanian leader Omar Torrijos sign the Panama Canal Treaty, September 7, 1977. Under the terms of the agreement, the United States turned over full control of the Canal on December 31, 1999.

nians: he demanded that the United States yield sovereignty over the Canal Zone back to Panama.

In 1977, after years of negotiations, Torrijos and President Jimmy Carter signed the Panama Canal and Neutrality Treaty, by which the United States pledged to fully turn the Canal over to Panama by the end of the century. The following year, Torrijos relinquished his post as president, but he retained power as head of Panama's National Guard. In 1981 he died in a plane crash, opening the way for another Panamanian military officer, Manuel Noriega.

In 1983 Noriega seized control of the National Guard (which he later renamed the Panamanian Defense Forces), making him the de facto leader of the country. Although he had been on the payroll of the Central Intelligence Agency, Noriega and the United States had a falling-out because of his involvement in drug trafficking and other illicit activities. U.S. officials indicted the Panamanian strongman on drug and racketeering charges in 1988.

In May 1989 Noriega nullified the results of presidential elections and declared himself Panama's head of state. The following December, U.S. forces invaded Panama to oust the general. The brief war claimed hundreds of lives and caused extensive damage to the country's capital. Noriega was captured and brought to the United States, where he was tried and convicted of drug trafficking, money laundering, and racketeering. After serving time in an American prison, Noriega was extradited to France in 2010 to face charges of money laundering brought by that country. Noriega was repatriated to Panama in 2011 and remains in prison there.

The Panama Canal, which employs about 9,000 people, directly generates more than $200 million for the national treasury each year and indirectly produces millions of dollars more. Moreover, the economy has generated a number of white-collar jobs for middle-class professionals, particularly in the financial services industry. Panama's gross national income per capita is second only to Costa Rica's among the countries of Central America. Still, economic problems plague Panama. In 2014 the poorest 20 percent of the nation's nearly 4 million people owned just over 3 percent of the nation's wealth. The richest 20 percent, in contrast, owned nearly 60 percent of it.

In 2002, citizens of Panama took to the streets to protest government corruption. A year later, public services were effectively shut down by a national workers' strike over the management of social security. President Martin Torrijos vowed reforms, but in 2005 another wave of strikes took place to protest the social security system.

As the 100th anniversary of the Panama Canal neared, plans were made to upgrade the canal so that larger container ships could pass through it. Construction on the expansion project began in 2011; although there have been many delays, the project is expected to be completed by 2017.

Juan Carlos Varela was elected president of Panama in 2014. Soon after he entered office, he offered temporary amnesty to any criminal gangs that agreed to give up their arms and sever ties to organized crime.

Costa Rica: Rewards of Peace

"Costa Rica," a historian once wrote, "does not seem to belong in Central America." This small nation—bordered by Panama to

Arenal, a volcano, is a well-known landmark in Costa Rica

the south and Nicaragua to the north—has avoided the disastrous social and political problems that have plagued its neighbors. Unlike the other Central American countries, Costa Rica has enjoyed a stable democracy since the late 1800s (marred only by a few brief periods of political unrest). Military interference in government and society has not been a major issue. In fact, Costa Rica abolished its national army in 1950.

Costa Rica's 4.7 million people enjoy Central America's highest per capita income, and the distribution of wealth is considerably more equal than in other Central American countries. Land ownership is high. The poverty rate is the lowest in the region. Unemployment is around 8 percent, comparable with recent rates in the United States. Costa Rica's educational system is excellent: more than 95 percent of the population can read and write.

Because of its stability, relative prosperity, and neutrality, Costa Rica has sometimes been called the Switzerland of the

Americas. It shares something else with that alpine country of Europe: Costa Rica is a land of breathtaking beauty that has become a popular destination for tourists. Unspoiled beaches on the Caribbean and Pacific coasts, lush rain forests, volcanic peaks, and an abundance of national parks are some of the country's major attractions.

Because of its stable society, peaceful history, and high education levels, Costa Rica has also benefited from foreign investment. Its economy has developed a strong technology sector, exporting electronics, for example. Nevertheless, the Costa Rican economy still depends largely on agriculture, particularly key crops such as bananas, coffee, and pineapples. Recent low prices for these crops have hurt.

Despite its lack of an army and its neutrality in foreign affairs, Costa Rica has been a regional leader. Oscar Arias Sánchez, who served as Costa Rica's president from 1986 to 1990, took the lead in promoting diplomatic solutions to Central America's conflicts and crafted a peace plan for Nicaragua. Arias won the Nobel Peace Prize in 1987 for his efforts.

Later leaders, however, did not fare so well. Three former presidents—Jose Maria Figueres, Miguel Angel Rodriguez, and Rafael Angel Calderon—were investigated for corruption in 2004. Four years later, Calderon was sentenced to five years in prison. In 2010, Costa Rica elected its first woman president, Laura Chinchilla. Luis Guillermo Solis succeeded her in 2014.

Because of Costa Rica's good social, political, and economic conditions, emigration has been comparatively low. Costa Ricans in the United States number fewer than 90,000.

Belize: English Influences

Belize is Central America's youngest nation, having gained independence in 1981, as well as its most sparsely populated, with only about 351,000 people as of 2014.

The history of this country—which lies along the Caribbean Sea east of Guatemala and southern Mexico—differs markedly from that of the rest of Central America. It was colonized not by

Many tourists visit Belize to see its Mayan ruins.

Spain, but by England (throughout much of its modern history it was known as British Honduras). The first British colonists, logwood cutters from Jamaica, are believed to have arrived in the late 1630s. The area also became home to British buccaneers who preyed on Spanish shipping. Despite frequent attacks by the Spanish throughout the 18th century, the British managed to keep control of the land. Today the official language of Belize is English, and the country probably has more in common with Jamaica and Barbados than with its Central American neighbors. The recent history of Belize has been fairly peaceful, although a border dispute with Guatemala delayed the country's independence by two decades.

By area, Belize is only slightly larger than El Salvador, Central America's smallest country. But despite its small size, the country is ethnically and culturally diverse. Belizeans share black, white, Mayan, and Garifuna (mixed black and Carib and

Arawak Indian) roots, and in addition to English, languages spoken in Belize include Spanish, Mayan, Creole, and Garifuna.

Poor by the standards of the industrialized world, Belize is about average for the region: it ranked third among the Central American countries in income per capita in 2014. More than 15 percent of Belizeans are unemployed. In 2011, Belize was added to the U.S. list of countries that are major producers or traffickers of drugs.

Although Great Britain has been accused of exploiting the natural resources of its former colony, it also passed on fairly strong political and educational institutions. To some degree this has mitigated the effects of poverty and given Belize fairly good prospects for future stability and economic development.

Belize's main exports are sugar and citrus, but tourism and related service industries are its largest earners. Its beaches on the Gulf of Mexico make it a popular tourist destination, especially among those seeking to explore the country's natural wonders. Belize is a popular stop for cruise ships, but their arrivals in turn have threatened habitats of native mammals and birds. Belize also contains many Mayan sites.

 Text-Dependent Questions

1. What is an isthmus?
2. What is the major export of El Salvador?
3. When was the Panama Canal constructed?

 Research Project

Find newspaper of magazine reports from the mid 1970s about the Panama Canal and Neutrality Treaty. Write a three to five paragraph opinion paper either supporting or disagreeing with the Treaty, using specific arguments leaders and citizens made at the time.

3 A BRIEF HISTORY OF IMMIGRATION TO NORTH AMERICA

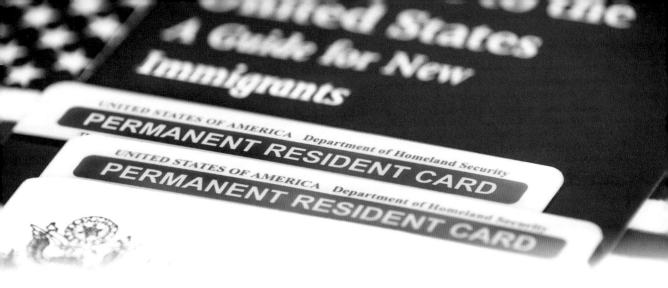

Immigration to the United States has been characterized by openness punctuated by periods of restriction. During the 17th, 18th, and 19th centuries, immigration was essentially open without restriction, and, at times, immigrants were even recruited to come to America. However, during the late 19th and early 20th centuries, American government policies restricted immigration, often based on racial or ethnic standards.

The Chinese Exclusion Act of 1882, which was not repealed until 1943, specifically prevented Chinese people from becoming U.S. citizens and did not allow Chinese laborers to immigrate until the 1950s. An agreement with Japan in the early 1900s prevented most Japanese immigration to the United States. The Immigration Act of 1924 set annual quotas on immigrants that were specifically designed to keep out southern Europeans, such as Italians and Greeks.

While the new law was rigid, the U.S. Department of State's restrictive interpretation directed consular officers overseas to be even stricter in their application of the "public charge" provision. Consuls were to deny a visa to any applicant they believed might ever be unable to support himself or his family.

In the early 1900s, more than one million immigrants a year came to the United States. In 1930—the first year of the

◀A customs post on the border between Honduras and El Salvador.

national-origin quotas—approximately 241,700 immigrants were admitted. But under the State Department's strict interpretations, only 23,068 immigrants entered during 1933, the smallest total since 1831. Later these restrictions prevented many Jews in Germany and elsewhere in Europe from escaping what would become the Holocaust. At the height of the Holocaust in 1943, the United States admitted fewer than 6,000 refugees.

The Displaced Persons Act of 1948, the nation's first refugee law, allowed many refugees from World War II to settle in the United States. The law put into place policy changes that had already seen immigration rise from 38,119 in 1945 to 108,721 in 1946 (and later to 249,187 in 1950). One-third of those admitted between 1948 and 1951 were Poles, with ethnic Germans forming the second-largest group.

The 1952 Immigration and Nationality Act is best known for its restrictions against those who supported communism or anarchy. However, the bill's other provisions were quite restrictive and were passed over the veto of President Truman. The 1952 act retained the national-origin quota system for the Eastern Hemisphere. The Western Hemisphere continued to operate without a quota and relied on other qualitative factors to limit immigration. Moreover, during that time, the Mexican bracero program, from 1942 to 1964, allowed millions of Mexican agricultural workers to work temporarily in the United States.

The 1952 act set aside half of each national quota to be

 Words to Understand in This Chapter

amnesty—broadly, a pardon; in immigration terms, the widespread granting of legal status to undocumented immigrants.

asylum—protection given by one country to refugees from another country.

deportation—the forced removal from a country of an individual by immigration authorities.

dictatorship—a government controlled by a ruler with absolute power.

exodus—a large departure of people.

divided among three preference categories for relatives of U.S. citizens and permanent residents. The other half went to aliens with high education or exceptional abilities. These quotas applied only to those from the Eastern Hemisphere.

A Halt to the National-Origin Quotas

The Immigration and Nationality Act of 1965 became a landmark in immigration legislation by specifically striking the racially based national-origin quotas. It removed the barriers to Asian immigration, which later led to opportunities to immigrate for many Filipinos, Chinese, Koreans, and others. The Western Hemisphere was designated an annual ceiling of 120,000 immigrants but without a preference system or per country limits. Modifications made in 1978 ultimately combined the Western and Eastern Hemispheres into one preference system and one ceiling of 290,000 immigrants per year.

The 1965 act built on the existing system—without the national-origin quotas—and gave somewhat more priority to family relationships. It did not completely overturn the existing system but rather carried forward essentially intact the family immigration categories from the 1959 amendments to the

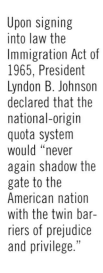

Upon signing into law the Immigration Act of 1965, President Lyndon B. Johnson declared that the national-origin quota system would "never again shadow the gate to the American nation with the twin barriers of prejudice and privilege."

Immigration and Nationality Act. Even though the text of the law prior to 1965 indicated that half of the immigration slots were reserved for skilled employment immigration, in practice, Immigration and Naturalization Service (INS) statistics show that 86 percent of the visas issued between 1952 and 1965 went for family immigration.

A number of significant pieces of legislation since 1980 have shaped the current U.S. immigration system. First, the Refugee Act of 1980 removed refugees from the annual world limit and established that the president would set the number of refugees who could be admitted each year after consultations with Congress.

Second, the 1986 Immigration Reform and Control Act (IRCA) introduced sanctions against employers who "knowingly" hired undocumented immigrants (those here illegally). It also provided amnesty for many undocumented immigrants.

Third, the Immigration Act of 1990 increased legal immigration by 40 percent. In particular, the act significantly increased the number of employment-based immigrants (to 140,000), while also boosting family immigration.

Fourth, the 1996 Illegal Immigration Reform and Immigrant Responsibility Act (IIRAIRA) significantly tightened rules that permitted undocumented immigrants to convert to legal status and made other changes that tightened immigration law in areas such as political asylum and deportation.

Fifth, in response to the September 11, 2001, terrorist attacks, the USA PATRIOT Act and the Enhanced Border Security and Visa Entry Reform Act tightened rules on the granting of visas to individuals from certain countries and enhanced the federal government's monitoring and detention authority over foreign nationals in the United States.

New U.S. Immigration Agencies

In a dramatic reorganization of the federal government, the Homeland Security Act of 2002 abolished the Immigration and Naturalization Service and transferred its immigration service and enforcement functions from the Department of Justice into a new Department of Homeland Security. The Customs Service, the Coast Guard, and parts of other agencies were also transferred into the new department.

The Department of Homeland Security, with regards to immigration, is organized as follows: The U.S. Customs and Border Protection division (CPB) contains Customs and Immigration inspectors, who check the documents of travelers to the United States at air, sea, and land ports of entry; and Border Patrol agents, the uniformed agents who seek to prevent unlawful entry along the southern and northern border. The and U.S. Immigration and Customs Enforcement division (ICE) employs investigators, who attempt to find undocumented immigrants inside the United States, and Detention and Removal officers, who detain and seek to deport such individuals. The U.S. Citizenship and Immigration Services (USCIS) is where people go, or correspond with, to become U.S. citizens or obtain permission to work or extend their stay in the United States.

Following the terrorist attacks of September 11, 2001, the Department of Justice adopted several measures that did not require new legislation to be passed by Congress. Some of these measures created controversy and raised concerns about civil liberties. For example, FBI and immigration agents detained for months more than 1,000 foreign nationals of Middle Eastern descent and refused to release the names of the individuals. It is alleged that the Department of Justice adopted tactics that discouraged the detainees from obtaining legal assistance. The Department of Justice also began requiring foreign nationals from primarily Muslim nations to be fingerprinted and questioned by immigration officers upon entry or if they have been living in the United States. Those involved in the September 11 attacks were not immigrants—people who become permanent residents with a right to stay in the United States—but holders of temporary visas, primarily visitor or tourist visas.

In 2004, President Bush pushed for immigration reform, specifically a guest worker program that would have allowed for

President George W. Bush, flanked by members of Congress, signs the Enhanced Border Security and Visa Entry Reform Act, May 14, 2002. The legislation, passed in response to the September 11, 2001, terrorist attacks on the United States, tightened rules on the granting of visas.

immigrants to obtain temporary work visas in the U.S. After that failed to gain traction, he again tried in 2007 to create a path for current immigrants to gain legal status and temporary work permits. This legislation would also have included tighter border security. Following outcry from conservatives, the plan failed and the legislation did not pass the Senate.

In 2001, senators Orrin Hatch (R-UT) and Richard Durbin (D-IL) and Representatives Howard Berman (D-CA) and Chris Cannon (R-UT) introduced the bi-partisan Development, Relief, and Education of Alien Minors (DREAM) Act. The DREAM Act would allow immigrants who were brought here illegally as young children (15 and under) to have a path to citizenship in adulthood. This multi-phase, 6-year plan has met with resistance by some conservatives and has not yet passed, even after a renewed push in 2010. Several states have adopted their own version, but they vary.

In 2012, President Obama created the Deferred Action for Childhood Arrivals (DACA) policy. Under DACA, people under the age of 31 who arrived in the U.S. before they were 16 can qualify for legal presence, which differs from legal status. Legal presence allows the person to be in the U.S. legally, receive a Social Security number and driver's license (with the exception of Nebraska residents), and apply for employment authorization. DACA protection is good for two years and can be renewed after that. DACA does not result in citizenship or permanent residency for these immigrants, as the DREAM Act would.

Today, the annual percentage of legal immigrants who constitute the overall U.S. population is higher than it has been at nearly any other period in U.S. history. For example, in 1970 immigrants made up approximately 4.7 percent of the total U.S. population. Today, the percentage is about 13.1, equaling the 13 percent or higher that prevailed in the country from 1860 to 1930. As has been the case previously in U.S. history, some people argue that even legal immigration should be lowered. These people maintain that immigrants take jobs native-born Americans could fill and that U.S. population growth, which immigration contributes to, harms the environment. In 1996 Congress voted against efforts to reduce legal immigration.

Most immigrants (900,000 to one million annually) enter the United States legally. But over the years the undocumented (illegal) portion of the population has increased to about 3.4 percent of the U.S. population—approximately 11 million people in all.

Today, the legal immigration system in the United States contains many rules, permitting only individuals who fit into certain categories to immigrate—and in many cases only after waiting anywhere from one to ten years or more, depending on the demand in that category. The system, representing a compromise among family, employment, and human rights concerns, has the following elements:

> A U.S. citizen may sponsor for immigrations an immediate relative, defined as a spouse, unmarried minor child (under 21 years old) or parent (petitioner must be at least 21). An unlimited number of visas is available for these immediate relatives.
>
> A limited number of visas are available for adult children (married or unmarried) and siblings of U.S. citizens (citizens must be at least 21 to petition for a sibling) and for spouses and unmarried children (minor and adult) of lawful permanent residents (LPRs, or green card holders) of the U.S.

A foreign national may immigrate if he or she gains an employer sponsor.

An individual who can show that he or she has a "well-founded fear of persecution" may come to the country as a refugee—or be allowed to stay as an asylee (someone who receives asylum).

Beyond these categories, essentially the only other way to immigrate is to apply for and receive one of the "diversity" visas, which are granted annually by lottery to those from "underrepresented" countries. There is a limited number of these visas, and in 2013 President Obama set a worldwide refugee ceiling at 70,000. Those 70,000 are allocated to various regions of the globe, with 5,000 for people from Latin America and the Caribbean.

In 1996 changes to the law prohibited nearly all incoming immigrants from being eligible for federal public benefits during their first five years in the country. Refugees were mostly excluded from these changes. Immigrants who entered the U.S. before August 22, 1996 are grandfathered in, but those who entered after that date face a list of restrictions. With a few exceptions, these immigrants are only eligible for Social Security, Supplemental Nutrition Assistance (SNAP), Medicaid and other benefits if they meet specific criteria that differ from program to program. In addition, families who sponsor relatives must sign an affidavit of support showing they can financially take care of an immigrant who falls on hard times.

A Short History of Canadian Immigration

In the 1800s, immigration into Canada was largely unrestricted. Farmers and artisans from England and Ireland made up a significant portion of 19th-century immigrants. England's Parliament passed laws that facilitated and encouraged the voyage to North America, particularly for the poor.

After the United States barred Chinese railroad workers from settling in the country, Canada encouraged the immigration of Chinese laborers to assist in the building of Canadian railways. Responding to the racial views of the time, the Canadian Parliament began charging a "head tax" for Chinese and South

Asian (Indian) immigrants in 1885. The fee of $50—later raised to $500—was well beyond the means of laborers making one or two dollars a day. Later, the government sought additional ways to prohibit Asians from entering the country. For example, it decided to require a "continuous journey," meaning that immigrants to Canada had to travel from their country on a boat that made an uninterrupted passage. For immigrants or asylum seekers from Asia this was nearly impossible.

As the 20th century progressed, concerns about race led to further restrictions on immigration to Canada. These restrictions particularly hurt Jewish and other refugees seeking to flee persecution in Europe. Government statistics indicate that Canada accepted no more than 5,000 Jewish refugees before and during

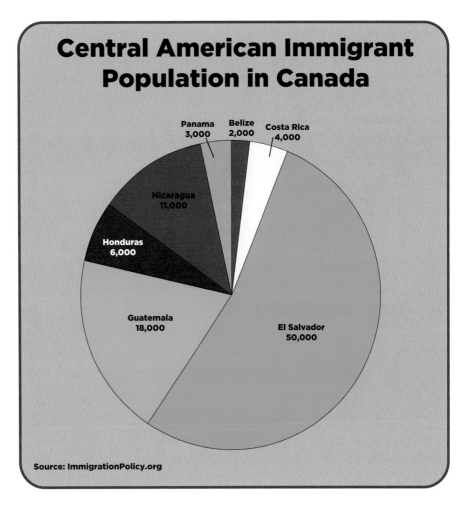

the Holocaust.

After World War II, Canada, like the United States, began accepting thousands of Europeans displaced by the war. Canada's laws were modified to accept these war refugees, as well as Hungarians fleeing Communist authorities after the crushing of the 1956 Hungarian Revolution.

The Immigration Act of 1952 in Canada allowed for a "tap on, tap off" approach to immigration, granting administrative authorities the power to allow more immigrants into the country in good economic times, and fewer in times of recession. The shortcoming of such an approach is that there is little evidence immigrants harm a national economy and much evidence they contribute to economic growth.

In 1966 the government of Prime Minister Lester Pearson introduced a policy statement stressing how immigrants were key to Canada's economic growth. With Canada's relatively small population base, it became clear that in the absence of newcomers, the country would not be able to grow. The policy was introduced four years after Parliament enacted important legislation that eliminated Canada's own version of racially based national-origin quotas.

In 1967 a new law established a points system that awarded entry to potential immigrants using criteria based primarily on an individual's age, language ability, skills, education, family relationships, and job prospects. The total points needed for entry of an immigrant is set by the Minister of Citizenship and Immigration Canada. The new law also established a category for humanitarian (refugee) entry.

The 1976 Immigration Act refined and expanded the possibility for entry under the points system, particularly for individuals seeking to sponsor family members. The act also expanded refugee and asylum law to comport with Canada's international obligations. The law established five basic categories for immigration into Canada: 1) family; 2) humanitarian; 3) independents (including skilled workers), who immigrate to Canada on their own; 4) assisted relatives; and 5) business immigrants (including investors, entrepreneurs, and the self-employed).

The Immigration and Refugee Protection Act, which took effect in 2002, made a series of modifications to existing Canadian immigration law. The act, and the regulations that followed, toughened rules on those seeking asylum and the process for removing people unlawfully in Canada.

The law modified the points system, adding greater flexibility for skilled immigrants and temporary workers to become permanent residents, and evaluating skilled workers on the weight of their transferable skills as well as those of their specific occupation. The legislation also made it easier for employers to have a labor shortage declared in an industry or sector, which would facilitate the entry of foreign workers in that industry or sector.

On family immigration, the act permitted parents to sponsor dependent children up to the age of 22 (previously 19 was the maximum age at which a child could be sponsored for immigration). The act also allowed partners in common-law arrangements, including same-sex partners, to be considered as family members for the purpose of immigration sponsorship. Along with these measures, the act also included provisions to address perceived gaps in immigration-law enforcement.

Central American Immigration Through the 1970s

In 1820, the year the U.S. government first began keeping immigration statistics, just two new arrivals were recorded from Central America. Immigration from the region remained low for many decades after this very modest start. In the period 1820–1830, for example, a total of 107 immigrants came from Central America; until the 20th century, the number never exceeded 1,000 per decade.

The first official record of Central American immigration to Canada dates to 1931, when the government counted three arrivals from the region. Some Central Americans had almost certainly moved to Canada before then, but they would have been listed under the "other" nationality category.

Throughout the 1900s, Latin Americans moved to the United States in significant numbers. For example, Mexican immigrants settled in the West and Southwest during the early part of the century. Puerto Ricans started arriving in large numbers in the 1950s, and Cubans flocked to the United States in the years after Fidel Castro came to power in 1959. But before 1960, Central Americans represented a small portion of the Hispanic immigrants to the United States.

During the 1960s, however, the number of Central American immigrants more than doubled from the previous decade, topping 100,000. Costa Ricans and Panamanians represented the largest immigrant groups from the region, though the nationalities that would later dominate—Salvadorans, Guatemalans, and Hondurans—weren't far behind in numbers.

The 1970s saw another expansion in Central American immigration, to about 130,000—though the rate of growth was much smaller than it had been during the previous decade. There were some important shifts in the demographics, however. Salvadorans now constituted the largest group of Central American immigrants by far.

Canada, meanwhile, continued to see a tiny amount of immigration from Central America. Between 1941 and 1970, just 893 Central Americans settled in the country. After the immigration reforms of 1967, Central American immigration to Canada increased, though the total numbers remained small. In the 1970s, only about 4,000 Central Americans, mostly from Guatemala and El Salvador, made Canada their new home.

The 1980s Immigration Explosion

During the 1980s, as violence engulfed Central America, emigration from the region exploded. Many of those fleeing the fighting, or the dismal economic situations the violence helped create, headed for Canada or the United States. Canada in the 1980s saw a 10-fold increase in Central American immigrants, to more than 40,000. The United States recorded half a million new immigrants from Central America in the 1980s, more than triple the number for the previous decade. It should be noted, however, that a part of this huge increase reflects changes in the law and INS recordkeeping rather than actual numbers of new immigrants. The 1986 Immigration Reform and Control Act offered amnesty to undocumented immigrants who had been living in the United States before 1982, and the INS counted amnesty recipients with new immigrants. Thus, the thousands of previously undocumented Central Americans who applied for and obtained amnesty inflated immigration statistics for several years in the late 1980s and early 1990s. For example, INS figures indicate that the number of Central American immigrants jumped from 37,000 in 1988 to 101,000 in 1989.

That is not to suggest that actual Central American immigration did not rise dramatically during the 1980s. War-torn El Salvador led the way. By some estimates, one of every five Salvadorans fled their country during the war years. The numbers of immigrants from other Central American countries also climbed steadily throughout the period. Thousands of Nicaraguans and Guatemalans, many of them poor peasants, fled the violence in their country. Many of these people entered the United States without permission. Hondurans, while not in the midst of a civil war, still suffered under a dictatorship and crushing poverty and also made their way to North America in significant numbers. The countries that a few decades before had been the largest sources of Central American immigrants—Costa Rica and Panama—did not see their numbers increase significantly. Belize saw a slight increase, but the totals stayed small.

As this immigrant wave hit the United States, the immigrant communities across the country grew and flourished. Before the 1980s the Pico-Union area of Los Angeles, for example, was widely known as a Mexican neighborhood. Today, the area is still home to many Mexicans but is defined by the distinctively Central American character provided by the large numbers of Salvadorans and Guatemalans who live and work in the gritty neighborhood. Other popular destinations for Central American immigrants included Miami, New York City, San Francisco,

Houston, Chicago, and Washington, D.C.

In Canada, small but strong Central American communities have developed in the nation's largest cities—Toronto, Montreal, and Vancouver—where most immigrants have settled.

Today, in the United States the top five states of settlement for immigrants from Central America are California, Texas, New York, Florida, and Maryland. In 2012 there were 2.7 million immigrants from the top three Central American countries for immigrants to the U.S.: El Salvador (1.3 million), Guatemala (880,000), and Honduras (536,000) in the U.S. That's a growth of 234 percent from 1990. The DHL estimates that of those immigrants, 1.6 million, or 60 percent, are in the U.S. illegally.

In Canada, the top five areas of settlement for immigrants from Central America are: Montreal, Quebec; Dorval, Quebec, Brossard, Quebec; Toronto, Ontario; and London, Ontario. In 2011, the three Central American countries that were the source of the most immigrants were El Salvador (43,500), Guatemala (15,000), and Nicaragua (9,000).

Immigrants Versus Refugees

A controversy erupted in the 1980s over U.S. policies dictating whether Central Americans arriving in the country qualified as economic immigrants or political refugees. Those in the latter group, defined as people fleeing political persecution and violence, are not subject to overall immigration limits and generally have an easier time being admitted into the country.

During the 1980s the United States typically granted refugee status to Nicaraguans while defining Guatemalans and Salvadorans as economic immigrants—even though all three countries were in the midst of civil wars. The only difference, critics charged, was that the U.S. government supported the regimes in power in Guatemala and El Salvador but opposed the Nicaraguan Sandinistas.

Many Americans objected to what they saw as the double standard that made it likely that a Nicaraguan refugee would quickly be given asylum, but a comparable Guatemalan or

Salvadoran might be detained and deported back to his or her country. In response, some activists started giving safe haven to undocumented immigrants from Guatemala and El Salvador. For its part, Canada recognized many Guatemalans and Salvadorans as refugees.

Since there was no "refugee processing" in the region (that is, U.S. officials did not interview potential refugees in Central America), the primary option chosen by Central Americans fleeing oppressive governments and violence in the 1970s and 1980s was to come to the United States and seek asylum. A class-action lawsuit filed in the 1980s on behalf of Guatemalan and Salvadoran asylum applicants asserted that the U.S. government was unfairly dismissing legitimate claims of persecution, in part because of U.S. support for the Guatemalan and Salvadoran governments. In 1990 the case—originally referred to as *American Baptist Churches of the U.S.A. v. Meese* but commonly called the *ABC* lawsuit—was finally settled. Under the terms of the settlement, all Salvadorans and Guatemalans in the United States as of 1990 were allowed to stay in the country and have another asylum interview.

As noted earlier, Congress in 1996 made it harder for individuals in the United States illegally to avoid deportation based on good standing in the community and years in the country. These provisions, as interpreted, adversely affected many Central Americans. In 1997, after much public attention to the issue, Congress passed the Nicaraguan and Central American Relief Act (NACARA). The law lowered the standard Salvadorans and Guatemalans—including those in the *ABC* class-action lawsuit— had to meet in order to remain in the country. NACARA gave Nicaraguans an even easier path to staying in the United States: generally speaking, it granted those in the country by 1995 permanent residence or green cards. Observers attributed this advantageous treatment to Nicaraguans' greater political influence among congressional Republicans.

Central American Immigration Today

By the 1990s, the Central American wars had begun to wind down, and all were over by the end of the decade. Nevertheless, immigration levels remained about the same during the 1990s as they had been during the 1980s, with some 500,000 Central Americans moving to the United States. Even in the absence of political violence, economic conditions throughout much of the region were difficult.

In 2000, according to the INS, 75,914 Central Americans immigrated to the United States. That was a little more than half the approximately 146,000 a year who came at the height of the exodus a decade earlier.

According to the Center for Immigration Studies, during the first decade of the 20th century, approximately 13.9 million

 The Sanctuary Movement

Many Guatemalans and Salvadorans fleeing the civil wars raging in their countries during the 1980s headed north to the United States. Thousands were admitted, but many were refused admission to the country or, if they entered illegally, were deported back home.

The Sanctuary Movement of the 1980s arose in response to U.S. immigration policies that did not recognize Guatemalans and Salvadorans fleeing war as political refugees. The movement started with a group of Arizona church leaders and soon spread across the country, being joined by synagogues and churches of every denomination. In just a few short years this loosely connected network had secretly placed thousands of undocumented Central Americans in safe houses around the United States.

Members of the Sanctuary Movement considered their actions a form of civil disobedience, likening their cause to that of the Underground Railroad, which during the 1800s helped escaped slaves flee to freedom in the Northern states. At its height, more than 500 places of worship agreed to shelter undocumented Central American immigrants.

The Sanctuary Movement's activity slowed after its leaders were arrested in 1985. Most were convicted but not jailed. The group largely disappeared after the Central American wars ended during the 1990s. However, when the regional ICE office in Phoenix, Arizona, began refusing to grant stays of deportation in 2014, some activists attempted to revive the Sanctuary Movement. By 2016, more than two dozen churches had signed on to the revived Movement.

Chicago is home to a large Guatemalan American community. Many live in the city's Humboldt Park section.

immigrants arrived in the U.S. This number makes 2000-2010 the highest decade of immigration in U.S. history. Nearly one-third of those immigrants came from Mexico. Central American immigrants made up about 1.2 million, with the majority coming from El Salvador.

In Canada, Central American immigration has never reached the levels it did in the United States. In 2011, fewer than 100,000 Central Americans made Canada their new home. Nearly half came from El Salvador. And while there are believed to be some 3 million people of Central American origin living in the United States they constitute only 5 to 7 percent of the country's Hispanic population, according to U.S. Census Bureau data.

Text-Dependent Questions

1. What does INS stand for?
2. The USA PATRIOT Act was created in response to what major terrorist event in the US?
3. What are the five basic categories for immigrant into Canada?

Research Project

Imagine you are the same age you are now but are a citizen living in one of the seven nations of Central America. Based on the requirements for immigration into both the US and Canada, which country would you be more likely to be able to enter? Support your answer in a three to five paragraph essay.

4 Making a New Life

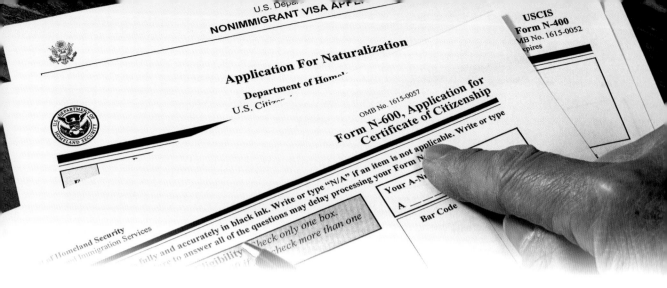

In his book *Strangers Among Us: How Latino Immigration Is Transforming America*, author Roberto Suro describes how the Houston area became home to thousands of Guatemalans. The process was fairly gradual, with new arrivals establishing themselves and then helping others to come. An illustrative example is the story of two Guatemalan women working as maids for an American family that was living in Guatemala. When the American family moved to Houston in the 1970s, the Guatemalan women went with them. A few years later, a young man from their hometown also moved to Houston and looked up the women, who helped him settle in and get a job at a supermarket. When this man's boss asked whether he knew of anyone who wanted a job, he sent for his relatives in Guatemala. Many other friends and relatives soon followed, attracted by the prospect of well-paying jobs and a peaceful life.

Magnet Communities

Immigrants face many challenges after they make the difficult choice to leave the land of their birth and move to the United States or Canada. They may speak little or no English and be unfamiliar with North American social and cultural customs.

◀Two Central American migrant workers harvest tobacco in Kentucky. Lacking a college education, language skills, and professional experience, the vast majority of Central American immigrants to the United States and Canada start out in low-wage work—for example, as agricultural laborers, landscapers, housekeepers, or janitors. But even these low-wage jobs are likely to represent a substantial improvement over employment prospects in their native countries.

They may not know how to go about applying for a job or enrolling their children in school. They may face discrimination. Even the weather may come as a shock: many people who hail from subtropical regions have never seen snow or experienced the bitter cold of a northern winter, for example.

It is not surprising, then, that most immigrants gravitate toward places where countrymen or women—or even relatives and friends—have already settled. The presence of familiar people, along with a familiar language and culture, can significantly ease the difficult transition to life in a strange new land. Friends, relatives, and compatriots form important support networks.

In 2000 the Immigration and Naturalization Service asked 22,578 new arrivals from El Salvador where they intended to live. About 30 percent said they were headed for Los Angeles, and 15 percent for Washington, D.C.—the cities with the largest Salvadoran communities in the country. Many also headed to Houston and Long Island, New York, which also have significant Salvadoran communities.

The relatively small numbers of Central Americans who immigrated to the United States in the decades before 1980 frequently settled in cities with established communities of Puerto Ricans, Mexicans, and Cubans, such as New York, Los Angeles, and Miami. There the newly arrived Central Americans formed tightly knit enclaves within the larger Hispanic communities. For example, English-speaking Panamanians, many of them descendants of West Indians, moved to Brooklyn's Bedford-Stuyvesant area starting in the 1950s. Salvadorans settled in the Adams-Morgan neighborhood of Washington, D.C., by the 1970s. Nicaraguans moved to Miami's Sweetwater area. A Guatemalan

 Words to Understand in This Chapter

immigrant—a person who moves to and settles in a new country.
remittance—money sent abroad.

Several thousand Central Americans—mainly Salvadorans, Guatemalans, and Hondurans—have settled in the Canadian port city of Vancouver, British Columbia.

community grew up in Chicago's Humboldt Park neighborhood.

These pioneers were more likely to be educated, middle-class professionals than were the Central Americans who arrived during the 1980s. But the later arrivals were drawn to the fledgling Central American communities that had started up in the 1960s and 1970s.

Central American neighborhoods are now spread from coast to coast. There are thriving communities of Salvadorans in San Francisco and Los Angeles, in addition to Washington, D.C.; Guatemalans in Los Angeles and Chicago; Nicaraguans in Miami; Panamanians in New York. In Canada, Salvadorans, Guatemalans, and Hondurans moved to Toronto, Montreal, and Vancouver.

On the other hand, immigrants from rural backgrounds may avoid cities altogether. Many seek work on farms and move to rural areas in California, Texas, or Florida. Some become migrant workers, moving from place to place according to the seasonal employment they can find. A migrant worker may spend the winter working in a cannery or food processing plant, start the spring picking strawberries, and keep working until apple-picking time in the fall.

Guatemalan immigrants of Mayan background who settled in Indiantown, Florida, starting in the mid-1980s are a good example. They came, many families with children, to escape the violence of their country's civil war. Many were from a particular group who speak a Mayan language called Kanjobal. In Indiantown, these families found jobs harvesting citrus and working in plant nurseries.

Central American immigrant communities such as the Kanjobal Mayans of Indiantown, or the many enclaves in large urban areas, develop informal support networks, which newcomers can turn to for help when they first arrive. The newcomers' neighbors may provide them places to stay, clothes, meals, and other necessities. They may help them find jobs.

But as greater numbers of Central Americans arrived during the 1980s, these community resources were stretched thin. The web of friends and neighbors that had always helped out could no longer keep up with the rapidly growing demands for shelter, food, and work.

Helping Hands

When the trickle of Central American immigrants to North America became a flood in the 1980s, a wide range of social service organizations stepped up to the challenge of helping new arrivals. Religious congregations and church-related organizations such as Catholic Charities provided shelter, food, legal assistance, and other forms of support to the immigrants.

Also, new organizations started up specifically to help these immigrants make the difficult transition. Among the largest was the Central American Refugee Center, known as CARECEN. The organization's first office opened in Washington, D.C., in 1981 to help the city's rapidly expanding Salvadoran community. CARE-

Los Angeles is the U.S. city with the largest population of Central Americans. Salvadorans and Guatemalans in particular have settled in L.A.'s Pico-Union neighborhood.

CEN began by offering legal aid to undocumented immigrants facing possible deportation, but its mission soon expanded. CARECEN began providing an array of services.

Today CARECEN's reach has expanded to many cities across the country, including Los Angeles, San Francisco, Houston, and New York. The nonprofit organizations offer new arrivals food, clothes, and assistance in finding places to live. The groups help to empower the immigrant community, offering a wide range of services, such as health care, language classes, and job training, along with cultural programs like art exhibits and plays.

The Los Angeles CARECEN runs a thriving community center in the city's Pico-Union area, home to many Central Americans. The center a valuable resource, providing services that range from after-school education for children to free legal support on immigration matters. The immigration and legal services often draw long lines of prospective clients in need of answers and advice. Other organizations across the country also help local Central American communities. Casa Guatemala was formed in Chicago to assist Guatemalans of Mayan descent. Project Honduras in Washington, D.C., has established a support network in that area.

Other organizations across the country also help local Central American communities. Casa Guatemala was formed in Chicago to assist Guatemalans of Mayan descent. Project Honduras in Washington, D.C., has established a support network in that area.

Some groups have sprung up in unlikely places. After

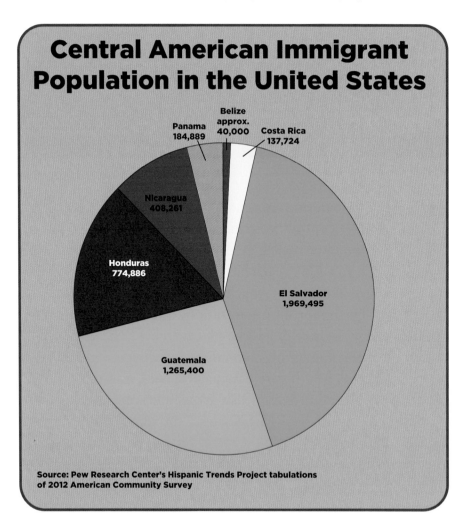

Central American Immigrant Population in the United States

Panama 184,889

Belize approx. 40,000

Costa Rica 137,724

Nicaragua 408,261

Honduras 774,886

El Salvador 1,969,495

Guatemala 1,265,400

Source: Pew Research Center's Hispanic Trends Project tabulations of 2012 American Community Survey

Hurricane Mitch slammed Honduras in 1998, a small group of volunteers in Oregon—where the Central American community is very small—organized to do their part for the relief effort. Begun by a native Honduran, the group raised thousands of dollars, and members even traveled to Honduras to help their adopted village of La Guacamaya recover and rebuild from the storm's devastation.

Getting Established

When a new immigrant arrives in the United States or Canada, the number one priority is finding shelter and food. New immigrants often live with friends or family or, if they are in a place where they don't know anyone to turn to for help, in temporary housing provided by local community groups or churches.

For most the next goal is finding work. Obviously those immigrants with a solid education, language skills, and professional experience have a better chance of finding well-paying jobs. Lacking these assets, the vast majority of Central American immigrants typically start out in low-wage work—for example, as housekeepers or janitors, gardeners or landscapers, roofers, farm workers, or dishwashers. Indeed, U.S. government statistics reveal that the percentage of Central American immigrants to the United States who are white-collar professionals and managers consistently lags behind the average for immigrants as a whole. But even a job paying minimum wage in the United States is likely to represent a substantial improvement over the work opportunities Central American immigrants can find in their native countries.

Most immigrants want to get better jobs and improve their quality of life. The key is language. After finding places to live and work, an important priority for many new arrivals is learning to speak English (or French, if they happen to move to a Canadian city such as Montreal where that is the predominant language). Although many colleges, community groups, and churches sponsor English-language classes for adults, mastering a new language is frequently a long and difficult process.

Those Left Behind

For many Central American immigrants, the knowledge that they are helping their loved ones back home makes more bearable the difficulties they face adjusting to life in a new country. Many immigrants set aside a portion of the money they earn to send to their families back home; and some, in fact, relocate to the United States or Canada for the express purpose of helping support loved ones in their country of origin. It is not unusual for men to immigrate alone, sending remittances—as cash payments sent home are called—to wives and children left behind. Because wages are substantially higher in the United States and Canada, every dollar remitted goes a long way.

Remittances by Central American immigrants have grown so much over the years that not only do individual families depend on the money to survive, but entire countries need the money to

 ## A Portrait of Chirilandria

This is the story of how an immigrant community is born and grows up.

Alexandria, Virginia, is a sprawling suburb outside Washington, D.C. During the 1980s, many Salvadorans fleeing civil war moved to Washington, but a handful settled in Alexandria.

Most of these immigrants hailed from a small southern town near the Pacific Ocean called Chirilagua. They settled where they could afford to live—in the poorest neighborhood in town, Arlandria. They struggled at the beginning, but they soon found jobs and made a fresh start.

These pioneers told their families and friends back in El Salvador about their newfound home. Gradually, more immigrants from Chirilagua moved into the community.

The first Salvadorans who moved to Alexandria helped out new arrivals, giving them places to stay and helping them find jobs. A new community began to emerge.

These immigrants attended church together. They played pickup soccer games in the park. They dined in restaurants serving Salvadoran cuisine. Before long, the neighborhood had been rechristened Chirilandria—a mix of Alexandria and Chirilagua. When a developer threatened to tear down the apartment buildings where so many Salvadorans had taken up residency, the tenants banded together and bought the whole complex, working hard to revitalize the area. Today, Alexandria's Salvadoran population is a valued asset to the community.

sustain their economies. Families in El Salvador, for example, received over 4 billion dollars from ex-patriot relatives in 2013 -- about one-sixth of the country's GDP that year. Nicaraguans sent home $1 billion, Guatemalans $5.5 billion, and Panamanians $760 million.

Sometimes an entire immigrant community will come together to raise money for their hometown. For example, a Salvadoran group in the Washington, D.C., area raised $300,000 to help their hometown of Chinameca. The Washington Post reported that these mostly working-class immigrants held parties, bake sales, and other fund-raisers to build a new clinic, laundry center, and school restroom in their native village.

"We feel the strain," one woman who worked two jobs to send money and medicine to her family told the Washington Post. "But at least we are allowing others to live better."

When natural disasters like hurricanes or earthquakes hit Central America, immigrants play an important role in pitching in to help. When Hurricane Mitch struck, killing thousands and leaving hundreds of thousands homeless, immigrants and immigrant groups coordinated relief efforts. They collected emergency supplies such as food and clothing, and, even though many were themselves struggling financially, they raised money to help their native countries.

 ## Text-Dependent Questions

1. What is Kanjobal?
2. What is CARECEN?
3. What 1998 hurricane devastated parts of Central America?

 ## Research Project

Imagine you are a new immigrant from Central America who has fled to the US after Hurricane Mitch. Write a letter to your neighbors back at home, explaining what challenges you face and how CARECEN has helped. Research CARECEN's website to find specific services they offer.

5 BEING CENTRAL AMERICAN IN NORTH AMERICA

When immigrants first arrive in a new land, they typically stand apart—often quite conspicuously—from the larger society. They might not speak the dominant language. Their culture, customs, and appearance may differ from what is common in the new country. Such differences don't just shape how citizens of the new country see the immigrants; they also define how the immigrants see themselves. A couple that has recently moved from Tegucigalpa to Los Angeles, for example, will almost certainly define themselves as Hondurans living in the United States rather than as Honduran Americans. And it is likely that many aspects of U.S. culture will strike them as strange.

Over time, however, this hypothetical couple will probably adapt to, and adopt, at least some facets of U.S. culture. And their children will be more at ease in the culture: even if their parents speak only Spanish at home, they will learn English from school, and through a variety of influences they will become familiar with customs, practices, and values common in the United States. Because of this, their sense of identity will likely differ from that of their parents: they'll probably define themselves as Honduran Americans.

◀ Scene from a Latino neighborhood in Los Angeles. Central American immigrants to the United States have retained many aspects of their cultures while gradually assimilating into mainstream U.S. society.

Of course, this is a vastly simplified picture of how immigrant groups blend in with the larger society over time—a process called assimilation. And it would be incorrect to suggest that assimilation means abandoning one set of cultural and social values for a new one. What most immigrants actually experience is a far more complex process: a melding of old and new cultures, of past and present with future aspirations. While they want to succeed in their new country, many immigrants also want to keep alive the heritage they cherish.

Diversity and National Pride

It would also be a mistake to talk about a monolithic "Central American culture," as if the seven countries of the region were indistinguishable. It is true that Central Americans have much in common. Their national histories were shaped largely by Spanish colonization. Spanish is the dominant tongue. Roman Catholicism, the most widely practiced religion, has had tremendous influence. Overall, mestizos—persons of mixed white and Amerindian ancestry—form the largest ethnic group.

But despite these generalities about the region, the countries of Central America are remarkably diverse. Belize, for example, was shaped by British rather than Spanish colonization, and its official language is English. Although Spanish is Nicaragua's official language, English and indigenous tongues are heard along the country's Atlantic coast. Many Panamanians are bilingual in English and Spanish. Four in 10 Guatemalans speak an

 Words to Understand in This Chapter

assimilation—the integration of a minority group into the mainstream culture.

indigenous—native to a country or region.

mestizo—a person of mixed European and Amerindian lineage.

quinceañera—a traditional party in Latin American societies to celebrate a young woman's 15th birthday.

Amerindian tongue. Fewer than half of all Belizeans are Catholics, El Salvador has a significant and growing Evangelical Protestant population, and a large number of Guatemalans practice an indigenous religion. Nine in 10 Hondurans claim mestizo heritage, while nearly 95 percent of Costa Ricans are white, one-quarter of Belizeans are Creoles (of mixed black and English ancestry), and 40 percent of Guatemalans descend directly from the Mayan Indians.

In addition to these differences, each of the seven countries of Central America has its own cultural and social traditions that set it apart. Each nation takes pride in its own food, music, and art.

Family at the Core

Central Americans—like Hispanics in general—tend to place family at the center of society. For many, a family may include the extended network of parents, children, grandparents, cousins, and even in-laws, sometimes living under the same roof. Traditionally, the father is the primary breadwinner and undisputed head of the family, while the mother's primary role is homemaker. Children are expected to be obedient and respectful.

However, traditional family roles often change for Central Americans who immigrate to the United States or Canada. For example, in many of these immigrant households, the women seek employment outside the home as a matter of economic necessity. This, in turn, tends to lead to greater independence for women than they might expect in the more socially conservative societies of their native countries.

Children of immigrants are often the quickest to adapt to their new homes. Because they attend school, they frequently are the first in their families to learn English. They, too, enjoy greater independence than they might have had in their own countries. Immigrant parents often worry that their children are becoming more rebellious and abandoning traditional cultural values.

"When children move decisively in this direction [learning English] while parents remain steeped in their own language and culture . . . communication across generations becomes more difficult and the resultant gap reduces parental authority," write Alejandro Portes and Ruben G. Rumbaut in their sociological study *Legacies: The Story of the Immigrant Second Generation.*

While encouraging their children to learn English and seize the opportunities that life in the United States or Canada offers, many immigrant parents strive to preserve the younger generation's ties to their culture. This may mean making sure that Spanish is spoken at home. It means going to church together. It means passing down stories about life in the old country.

It also means keeping alive important traditions such as the *quinceañera*. A *quinceañera* is an elaborate family party held when a girl turns 15, symbolizing and celebrating the girl's passage to womanhood. These celebrations are popular throughout Latin America. The festivities may feature music, dancing, and "royal courts" of girls dressed in elaborate gowns and boys in tuxedos. The occasion is cause for a community-wide celebration and includes extended families, friends, and neighbors. In many cases even families that are struggling financially save up money to throw a large *quinceañera* party for their daughters.

Spanish and English

Immigrants are under great pressure to learn English. Many will encounter limited opportunities for career advancement unless they learn the dominant language of their new country. And their children must overcome the language barrier if they want to succeed in school.

"Immigrants in a foreign land face a significant dilemma," write Portes and Rumbaut in *Legacies.* "The languages that they bring are closely linked to their sense of self-worth and national pride. On the other hand, these languages clash with the imperatives of a new environment that dictate abandonment of their cultural baggage and learning a new means of communication."

Even as they learn English, many Central Americans want to keep speaking Spanish at home. But as their children learn English in school, they sometimes wind up speaking "Spanglish," a blend

A Genius of Distinction

Ruben Blades makes some of the world's most electrifying and thought-provoking salsa music, but he has enjoyed success of many kinds over his distinguished and varied career.

Blades was born in 1948 in a poor neighborhood of Panama City. As a boy he dreamed of a career as a lawyer. He earned his law degree in Panama, but music was his life's great passion. In 1974 he moved from Panama to New York City to launch his career in salsa music, a distinctively Latin American style of dance music with roots in African music.

Blades became a popular songwriter and singer and enjoyed breakthrough solo success with his 1984 album *Buscando America* (Looking for America). What distinguishes Blades from most salsa musicians are his poetic and moving song lyrics, which explore complex social issues such as immigration and human rights with great honesty. In "Looking for America" he sings:

> "I am looking for America
> And I fear I will not find it....
> Living in dictatorships, I seek you
> But I do not find you....
> I am calling you, America."

Even as he pursued success as a musician, Blades made a mark in movies, playing roles in features such as *Crossover Dreams* and *The Milagro Beanfield War*. He also found the time to earn another law degree, from Harvard. Blades eventually returned to Panama to run for president in 1994. He campaigned on a platform of social and economic reform. Though he lost the election, he garnered more than 20 percent of the vote and gained attention for the issues he considers important.

The year 2004 was particularly successful for Blades. He won a Grammy Award for best salsa/meringue album (*Across 110th Street*) and began a five-year term as Panama's minister of tourism. Blades won the Harry Chapin Humanitarian Award in 2014 for charity work worldwide, and won another Grammy Award in 2015. He also joined the cast of the AMC network's show *Fear the Walking Dead* in 2015.

of both languages. This slangy speech is mostly harmless, but unfortunately children can end up speaking neither English nor Spanish well, mixing up vocabulary and syntax.

Keeping the Culture Alive

Central American immigrants preserve many customs from their native countries. By continuing to celebrate important holidays and sharing food from home, they foster community.

The Christmas season ranks as the biggest holiday of the year for many Central Americans. Families may construct elaborate Nativity scenes to mark the birth of Christ and pack the pews of their neighborhood church on Christmas Eve to attend midnight Mass.

Many Central American immigrants also continue to celebrate the feast day of their country's patron saint with special church services and community festivities. Costa Ricans, for example, honor the Virgin of the Angels every August 2.

Montreal, Canada's second-largest city, is home to more Central American immigrants than any other city in Canada. In 2013, about 50,000 immigrants from El Salvador lived in Canada.

Hondurans celebrate the Virgin of Suyapa's day on February 3. Nicaraguans mark the Feast of the Immaculate Conception on December 7 with a special holiday called La Purísima, during which families build altars to the Virgin Mary in their home and exchange gifts.

In areas with larger immigrant communities, families may even continue to honor the patron saints of their towns. In Los Angeles, for example, Kanjobal Mayans from San Miguel Acatán in Guatemala mark the feast day of St. Michael, the namesake of their hometown.

A sure sign that immigrants from a particular country have settled in an area is when restaurants and grocery stores selling food from home start to open in the neighborhood. Central America's cultural diversity is reflected in the wide range of foods eaten, though corn, beans, and tropical fruits are staples throughout the region. A Salvadoran seeking a taste of home might stop into a *pupusería* and order a plate of *pupusas*, a corn pancake filled with beans, cheese, and meat. A Nicaraguan might hanker for a corn and pork tamale called a *nacatamale*. A Panamanian might crave *sancocho*, a savory stew.

 Text-Dependent Questions

1. What is the most widely practiced religion in Central America?
2. What is a quinceañera?
3. What is a nacatamale?

 Research Project

Using the Internet, research the aspects of a quinceañera; what is served, what the girl might wear, why it is celebrated. Write a three to five paragraph essay about the common elements of a quinceañera.

6 Troubles in the Land of Opportunity

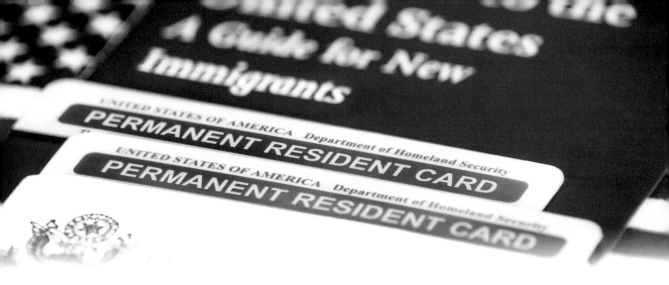

"Give me your tired, your poor, / Your huddled masses yearning to breathe free," reads the inscription at the base of the Statue of Liberty. For two centuries immigrants have been drawn to the United States by the promise of freedom, prosperity, a better life. And the United States has long defined itself as a nation of immigrants. But many immigrants have struggled to realize their dreams, and Americans haven't always been welcoming of newcomers.

Today hundreds of thousands of immigrants continue to arrive each year. Many who cannot get into the United States legally are prepared to do so illegally—sometimes even risking their lives in the process. These undocumented immigrants face extraordinary difficulties making their way in U.S. society—and, at the same time, they fuel anti-immigrant sentiment among some U.S. citizens.

The Undocumented

Establishing how many undocumented immigrants there are in the United States is difficult. Because they are subject to arrest and deportation if discovered, the undocumented carefully avoid coming into contact with official government agencies.

◀ A man of Hispanic heritage displays a half Salvadorian, half American flag at a pro-immigration rally in Boston, Massachusetts. More than 2.8 million Salvadorans, Guatemalans, and Hondurans were living in the United States illegally as of 2012, according to estimates by DHS Office of Immigration Statistics.

But the Department of Homeland Security (DHS) estimated the number of undocumented immigrants living in the United States as of the year 2012 at 11.4 million. The majority—an estimated 6.7 milion—came from Mexico. The number of Central Americans living in the country illegally was estimated at about 2 million, the great majority of whom were born in El Salvador, Guatemala, or Honduras.

No official statistics are available for how many Central Americans live in Canada illegally, but the number is thought to be small. Going to Canada extends the journey north by many hundreds of miles and requires an additional border crossing, with its accompanying risk of detection. Canadian officials estimate the total number of undocumented immigrants of all nationalities at around 75,000, though some experts believe the figure is considerably higher.

The Perilous Journey North

Most Central American undocumented immigrants make the long journey north through Mexico and sneak over the border to the United States. They travel by foot, train, car, or bus. However, some also enter the country legally as visitors or temporary residents and simply remain after their visa has expired. After they are in the United States, some obtain false documents that allow them to work and live without much suspicion.

The U.S. government devotes considerable resources to intercepting undocumented immigrants at the border, and to finding those who have already entered the country. Investigators of the

 Words to Understand in This Chapter

coyote—in Mexican and Central American slang, a professional smuggler of undocumented immigrants.

undocumented—not possessing the proper or necessary documents, especially as pertains to permission to work or live in another country.

U.S. Customs and Border Protection is the government agency that is responsible for preventing people from crossing the borders without proper documentation. Despite the penalties, many Central Americans are willing to risk their lives at potentially dangerous crossing areas along the U.S.-Mexico border for the chance to live in the United States.

Bureau of Immigration and Customs Enforcement attempt to discover undocumented immigrants in the interior of the country. The Bureau of Customs and Border Protection employs more than 21,000 Border Patrol agents in an attempt to keep out those who would enter the United States illegally. Along the 1,950-mile-long border with Mexico, the agents use helicopters, boats, all-terrain vehicles, and sophisticated surveillance equipment such as motion and infrared sensors. Each year, more than a million people are apprehended trying to cross the border without documents.

Yet, driven largely by economic need, the would-be immigrants keep coming. And in their attempts to avoid detection by the authorities, many try perilous routes—trekking through the deserts of the Southwest or swimming across rivers, for example. Some hire unscrupulous smugglers—referred to as coyotes or *polleros*—who promise to lead them safely into the United States but in many instances abandon, rob, or even kill their clients instead.

The business of smuggling people can be very lucrative—coyotes may charge more than $10,000 per person. In recent years U.S. officials have increasingly targeted these smugglers. In 2002 federal agents made headlines worldwide when they broke up a major crime ring accused of smuggling hundreds of Salvadoran and Guatemalan children into the United States. But the smugglers continue to ply their trade, sometimes with tragic results. In May 2003, for example, smugglers packed as many as 140

 ## Coyotes and Chickens

They travel in the dark of night—as many as a truckload, as few as one or two. They are willing to risk everything in pursuit of the American Dream.

With federal agents monitoring the borders, many immigrants seeking to enter the United States or Canada illegally hire professional smugglers called coyotes. The immigrants (referred to as *pollos*, or "chickens") hope that, like their namesake, the coyotes will be cunning, because eluding the authorities can be difficult.

In return for their promise to guide immigrants across the border, coyotes collect $2,000 to $5,000—and sometimes as much as $10,000—per person. (A Central American might need to spend hundreds or thousands of additional dollars to make the journey through Mexico to get near the border in the first place.)

Coyotes use various methods to avoid detection by border authorities. They may crowd groups into vans or freight trains or simply walk them across the border in extremely remote places, hiding from surveillance helicopters along the way. But it is not uncommon for coyotes to turn on their own clients after they have collected their fee. Many immigrants whom coyotes have abandoned in remote desert areas have died.

In recent years beefed-up border patrols have led to the capture of many coyotes. However, increased enforcement efforts—and the decision to focus on stopping illegal immigration near cities—have forced would-be immigrants to take routes through more remote areas, and in the process made the services of coyotes even more popular.

Mexican, Salvadoran, and Honduran immigrants inside a locked truck and drove them from Mexico into southern Texas. By the time they arrived in Victoria County, Texas, 18 were dead of asphyxiation, dehydration, or heatstroke, and at least one more died later in a hospital. Recently the annual death toll for immigrants trying to cross the border has exceeded 300.

However, desperate families continue to entrust their children to coyotes. A 2008 anti-trafficking law (as well as a backlog of immigration court cases) makes it unlikely that Central American children will be deported immediately if apprehended, and so many continue to take their chances in the U.S. system.

In June of 2014, the DHS announced a 90-day surge, called Operation Coyote, that was conducted by the Bureau of U.S. Immigration and Customs Enforcement (ICE) and Homeland Security Investigations (HIS). Operation Coyote targeted human smuggling operations in the Texas Rio Grande Valley. The operation resulted in the apprehension of nearly 400 smugglers and over $1 million.

In desert areas of the Southwest where many would-be immigrants attempt to make the dangerous crossing into the United States, some Americans have taken steps to prevent tragic deaths. For example, an organization called Humane Borders, which is based in Tucson, Arizona, has placed barrels of water along desert trails. In the 120-degree heat of the Arizona desert, immigrants on foot can easily succumb to dehydration.

Border Patrol agents criticize such efforts, saying they only encourage undocumented immigrants to risk their lives in dangerous and desolate areas. And some private citizens, angry at incidents of violence and lawlessness they blame on the stream of people crossing the border illegally and then moving through their communities, have organized themselves into private patrols to help apprehend undocumented immigrants.

Anti-immigrant Anger

Today an undercurrent of anti-immigrant sentiment—which has probably always run through society to a greater or lesser degree—can be discerned in certain quarters. Immigrants are often blamed for a variety of economic and social ills. A long-standing complaint is that new arrivals take jobs that would otherwise go to U.S. citizens. In the case of Central American immigrants, however, most of the jobs are low-paying positions that

Hispanic immigrants protest at a rally in Los Angeles in favor of laws that would create a legal path to citizenship for those who entered the country illegally.

employers frequently have difficulty filling with U.S.-born workers. Labor provided by Central American immigrants—for example, as fruit or vegetable pickers—actually benefits consumers and boosts the national economy.

Much anger directed at immigrants—particularly Hispanics—focuses on their perceived unwillingness or inability to learn to speak English. "Nothing seems to inflame advocates of the nation's Anglo-Saxon traditions so much as this issue of language," writes Juan Gonzalez in *Harvest of Empire*. Indeed, the United States has become a multilingual society—20 percent of U.S. households speak a language other than English at home, according to 2013 census data. Spanish is the most widespread of these other languages, and—to the dismay of English-only advocates—its use in the public sphere is growing. Anyone passing through a Latino neighborhood will see many store signs and billboard ads written in Spanish. Drivers can take licensing tests in Spanish. Teachers send home school reports in Spanish. Even census forms can be filled out in Spanish.

The idea of making English the official language of the United States has generated much discussion and controversy. The English-only movement dates to the early years of the century, when immigrants from Germany and Italy predominated. As Hispanic and Asian immigrants arrived in large numbers in the 1970s and 1980s, the movement enjoyed a revival.

English-only advocates say the move would promote national unity and ease the assimilation and social advancement of new immigrants. Opponents say English-only rules would violate freedom of speech rights and would unfairly target immigrants.

Congress has debated English-only legislation, and several states have passed similar measures, only to have them tied up in court battles. In recent years, the national movement seems to have lost political momentum, but several organizations still promote the English-only agenda.

In California—whose undocumented population is believed to be more than twice as large as that of any other state—anti-immigrant sentiment took the form of Proposition 187, which the state's voters passed in 1994. Proposition 187 would have cut off health and social services, including public schools, for undocumented immigrants and their children. It required government workers to ask people about their immigration status and to report those they suspected of being undocumented.

Supporters of the measure clearly were frustrated with illegal immigration in their state. They also were angry about the cost of providing public education, health care, and other social services to the undocumented. Opposition groups, however, claimed the law discriminated against Mexicans and Central Americans, who make up the majority of California's undocumented population.

A number of lawsuits prevented the law from ever taking effect. After much legal battling, a federal court struck down the

Lorenzo and Angelica Alvarez and their children, El Paso, Texas, 2000. About one in four Central Americans in the United States lives below the poverty line—a poverty rate more than twice as high as that of the general population.

Enrique's Odyssey

In 2002 the *Los Angeles Times* published a remarkable series of articles about Enrique, a Honduran teenager, and his perilous journey from his native town to the United States. Reporter Sonia Nazario retraced Enrique's steps, relating a compelling story that bears similarities to the stories of the 48,000 other children who enter the country illegally from Mexico and Central America each year.

"It is an epic journey for these children," said Nazario in an interview about the series. "They face gangsters, they face bandits, they face crooked police in Mexico, they face immigration authorities and they face the train . . . which is called the 'train of death.'"

Nazario describes Enrique's hard life in Honduras, where he lives in poverty and uses drugs. At 17 he leaves his town to find his mother, who left him behind when she moved to the United States 11 years before. He makes numerous failed attempts to cross Mexico by train, is nearly beaten to death on one trip, and encounters many other dangers before he finally makes it to the U.S. border. He swims across the Rio Grande with the help of a smuggler. The story concludes with Enrique reuniting with his mother but facing an uncertain future in the United States.

The articles drew significant reader response, raising awareness about the hardships so many undocumented immigrants face just making it across the border.

measure as unconstitutional. Proposition 187's largest significance may be its impact on electoral politics. While Pete Wilson, California's Republican governor, used his support of the measure to gain reelection, he alienated many in the Hispanic community, and some observers predicted a wider backlash against the Republican Party among Latino voters.

Approaches to the Undocumented

American public opinion remains sharply divided over what to do about illegal immigration. Some citizens call for stronger enforcement of the laws. Not only should security along the borders be tightened, they say, but efforts to track and deport undocumented immigrants should be stepped up dramatically.

Others, however, advocate a different approach. They believe that, with the countries south of the United States at peace, poverty is now the primary cause of illegal immigration. Thus, the best strategy for stemming the flow of undocumented immigrants, in this view, is for the United States to help develop the weak economies of Mexico and the Central American nations. At the same time, these people say, the government should both set up new mechanisms for people to enter the United States legally to work, and legalize the status of many of the undocumented who are already living in the country. Today it is estimated that nearly one-third of the undocumented have resided in the United States for a decade or longer.

Dreams Deferred

As Americans debate what to do about the undocumented and other immigration-related issues, immigrants themselves have their own set of issues to face. Many immigrants come to the United States or Canada to escape grinding poverty in their homeland—only to end up living a marginal existence in their new country as well.

Approximately one of every four Central Americans in the United States lives below the poverty line, according to the Census Bureau. That's more than twice the rate for the general population. In addition, more than half of all Central American immigrants in the United States lack health insurance. While sobering, these statistics don't necessarily tell the full story, however. Many impoverished Central American immigrants were also impoverished in their homelands, and their standard of living in the United States may be significantly better than it had been in their country of origin.

Many immigrants are traumatized by the violence and poverty they experienced in their home countries. These psychological stresses are another problem to overcome. Young children especially feel the impact. "The experience of civil war and death squads has produced a generation of children whose problems cannot be fitted into the routine of education," Earl Shorris wrote in his book, *Latinos: A Biography of the People.*

The United States Department of Education has identified a crisis with Hispanic students. Over the past two decades, public schools in certain areas of the country have struggled to accommodate many thousands of new students from Mexico and

Central America. A large proportion of these new students come from impoverished backgrounds; in their native countries they received little schooling, and they often speak little or no English. Many schools lack qualified teachers and resources to adequately address the educational needs of these disadvantaged children. Given these circumstances, it is perhaps not surprising that for Hispanic immigrant students, the dropout rate for 2011 was more than five times higher than the national average (46 percent versus 7.7 percent). Among the Hispanic immigrant students who drop out, 80 percent speak little or no English, according to a Department of Education study.

Unfortunately, without an education, the long-term prospects for children can be dim. "For most second generation Latinos . . . achieving middle class prosperity requires a long leap from the simple skills their parents bring with them to the advanced requirements of work in an information economy," writes Roberto Suro in *Strangers Among Us*.

Despite the obstacles and challenges, however, Central Americans continue to make the journey north. In many ways, being poor in the United States or Canada isn't as bad as being desperately poor in their native countries. The immigrants hold out the hope that if they work hard enough, they may wind up living the dream.

 ## Text-Dependent Questions

1. What is inscribed on the base of the Statue of Liberty?
2. What is a coyote?
3. Approximately how many Central Americans in the United States lives below the poverty line?

 ## Research Project

Using the library or the Internet, find articles written about Proposition 187 in 1993 and 1994. Write a three to five paragraph essay outlining the arguments for and against Proposition 187.

7 A FUTURE OF POSSIBILITIES

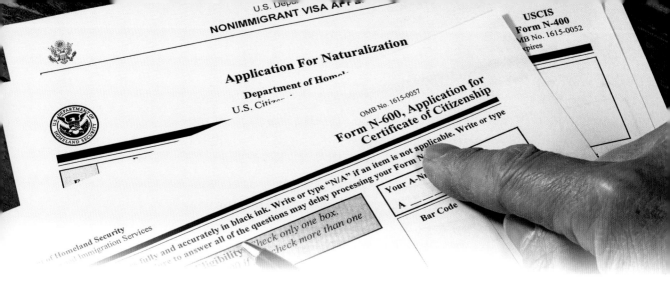

Central American immigration to the United States leveled off considerably following the highs of the 1980s and early 1990s. The total number of Central American legal immigrants rose from about 35,000 in 1998 to 76,000 in 2001. In 2013, according to the DHS, the figure stood at approximately 44,000. It is likely that as long as Central America remains beset with economic instability and the social consequences of poverty, significant numbers of people will want to leave to find a better life elsewhere.

Central American immigration to Canada, meanwhile, has been far more stable. After hitting an all-time high of close to 13,000 in 1991, the numbers dropped off considerably, averaging just over 4,000 per year over the following decade.

A Growing Community

Central American communities are flourishing in cities across the United States and Canada. As time passes, these neighborhoods are growing and maturing. At the same time, individuals who find success often move out of the inner cities and into suburban homes. In short, Central Americans have become part of the fabric of North America.

What does the future hold for this vibrant community?

◀ The vibrant and growing community of Central Americans in the United States—and, to a lesser degree, Canada—will continue to change the face of North America as the 21st century unfolds.

Demographic trends suggest that Central Americans' presence in the United States will only increase.

The U.S. census of 2010 counted more than 50 million people who identified as Hispanic or Latino, about 16 percent of the nation's entire population. That total included 3.9 million Central Americans. By 2050 there could be more than 100 million Hispanics, slightly more than 30 percent of the population. By the beginning of the next century, the number of Hispanics in the United States could rise to nearly 200 million—one of every three Americans. If Central Americans are represented in the same proportion 100 years from now as today, there could be more than 15 million in the United States.

These population projections may seem remarkable, but consider history. The population of Hispanics in the United States nearly quadrupled from 1970 to 2000.

"This demographic shift is so massive," writes Juan Gonzalez in *Harvest of Empire*, "it is transforming the ethnic composition of the country and challenging key aspects of its accepted national identity, language, culture, and official history, a seismic social change. . . ."

Government Initiatives

With the failure of the DREAM Act to pass in the United States on a national level, a number of states adopted their own variations. As a national initiative, DACA was introduced in 2012 by President Obama. The Deferred Action for Childhood Arrival offers a two-year protection from deportation for people under the age of 31 who arrived in the U.S. when they were less than

 Words to Understand in This Chapter

initiative—a new plan for addressing a particular problem or need.
demographic—information relating to the population or groups within the population.

Passage of the Dominican Republic-Central America Free Trade Agreement (DR-CAFTA) in 2009 may affect immigration from Central America, as businesses such as this coffee mill in El Salvador expand and hire more workers.

16 years old. As this book was being written, an injunction was preventing DACA from being extended to 3 years.

In August of 2004, the United States entered into a Free Trade Agreement with five Central American countries and the Dominican Republic. By 2009, the agreement, known as DR-CAFTA (sometimes CAFTA-DR), was fully in effect. The five Central American countries involved are El Salvador, Honduras, Nicaragua, Guatemala, and Costa Rica. The agreement is intended to have economic benefits for all the countries involved—but it especially to help Central America's poorer nations to expand and develop their economies. Indeed, since the agreement went into effect, two-way trades between the U.S. and six countries involved has increased over 71 percent, from $35 billion in 2005 to $60 billion in 2013.

A lot of controversy surrounds this free trade agreement, however. Some argue that by opening trade, the Central

Central American immigrants play a soccer game in a New York park.

American countries involved will lower environmental and wage standards in a race to sell to the U.S. On the opposing view, others argue that increasing trade to these six countries serves to reduce the demand for U.S.-manufactured goods.

While Canada still has relatively few Central Americans, the country is faced with an aging population and a shrinking labor force. Due to these factors, the country is stepping up efforts to draw more immigrants. The government hopes to attract more skilled workers from foreign countries and relocate them in cities and towns across the country.

Whether these Canadian and U.S. policy initiatives succeed or whether population projections turn out to be accurate, Hispanics will have a huge impact on North America over the coming century. In the United States particularly, they have already established a powerful presence in politics, mass media, and popular culture. And Central Americans, given their own growing numbers, can be expected to play a critical role in the larger Latino community and the nation as a whole.

 ## Text-Dependent Questions

1. Approximately how many people immigrated from Central America to Canada in 1991?
2. What percent of the US population identified as Hispanic or Latino in the 2010 census?
3. What is DR-CAFTA?

 ## Research Project

Using the library or the Internet, research the DREAM Act. Write a three to five paragraph essay outlining the arguments for and against it.

Famous Central Americans

HORACIO AGUIRRE (1926–) Raised in Nicaragua, he founded Miami-based *Diario las Américas*, a leading Spanish-language newspaper.

RUBEN BLADES (1948–) Born in Panama, this groundbreaking salsa musician moved to the United States in the 1970s to escape political oppression. His 2014 album, *Tangos*, won a Grammy for Best Latin Pop Album.

JORDANA BREWSTER (1980–) Born in Panama, she is an actress who is best known for her role as Mia Toretto in the *Fast and Furious* movie franchise.

CHRISTY TURLINGTON BURNS (1969–) Born in California to a Salvadoran mother, this supermodel has graced the covers of countless fashion magazines. She is active with Salvadoran charities and has raised money to help rebuild the country.

ROD CAREW (1945–) Born in Panama, baseball star Carew collected more than 3,000 hits in an 18-year career with Minnesota and California. He is a member of the National Baseball Hall of Fame.

ROSEMARY CASALS (1948–) Born in San Francisco to Salvadoran immigrants, Casals was a professional tennis player. She is a member of the International Tennis Hall of Fame.

FRANKLIN R. DIAZ-CHANG (1950–) Born in Costa Rica, Diaz-Chang moved as a teenager to the United States and became a physicist. He joined NASA and flew seven missions as a space shuttle astronaut.

AMERICA FERRERA (1984–) Born in Los Angeles to Honduran immigrants, Ferrera is an actress and social activist. She starred in Ugly Betty from 2006-2010 and has been an ambassador for Save the Children.

JOSE RENE "J. R." MARTINEZ (1983–) Born in Louisiana to a Salvadoran mother, this U. S. Army veteran became a motivational speaker after he was severely burned by a roadside bomb in Iraq. He is a best-selling author and was the season 13 winner of ABC's *Dancing With the Stars*.

JOSÉ QUINTERO (1924–1999) Born in Panama, he moved to the United States as a college student and became a Broadway theater director. He was twice awarded the Tony, the theater's highest honor.

DAPHNE RUBIN-VEGA (1969–) Born in Panama and raised in New York, the actress and singer made her Broadway stage debut starring in Rent, for which she earned a Tony nomination.

Series Glossary of Key Terms

assimilate—to adopt the ways of another culture; to fully become part of a different country or society.

census—an official count of a country's population.

deport—to forcibly remove someone from a country, usually back to his or her native land.

green card—a document that denotes lawful permanent resident status in the United States.

migrant laborer—an agricultural worker who travels from region to region, taking on short-term jobs.

naturalization—the act of granting a foreign-born person citizenship.

passport—a paper or book that identifies the holder as the citizen of a country; usually required for traveling to or through other foreign lands.

undocumented immigrant—a person who enters a country without official authorization; sometimes referred to as an "illegal immigrant."

visa—official authorization that permits arrival at a port of entry but does not guarantee admission into the United States.

Further Reading

Booth, John A.; Christine J. Wade; and Thomas W. Walker. *Understanding Central America: Global Forces, Rebellion, and Change*. Sixth ed. Boulder: Westview Press, 2014.

Foster, Lynn. *A Brief History of Central America*. New York: Facts On File, 2000.

Fox, Geoffrey E. *Hispanic Nation: Culture, Politics and the Constructing of Identity*. Tucson: University of Arizona Press, 1997.

Gonzalez, Juan. *Harvest of Empire: A History of Latinos in America*. Rev. ed. New York: Penguin Books, 2011.

Jonas, Susanne, and Rodriguez, Nestor. *Guatemala-U. S. Migration: Transforming Regions*. Austin: University of Texas Press, 2015.

Martinez, Oscar. *The Beast: Riding the Rails and Dodging Narcos on the Migrant Trail*, trans. Daniela Maria Ugaz. New York: Verso, 2013.

Menchu, Rigoberta. *I, Rigoberta Menchu: An Indian Woman in Guatemala*. New York: Verso Books, 1994.

Merino, Noel. *Illegal Immigration*. San Diego: Greenhaven Press, 2015.

Olmos, Edward J.; Lea Ybarra; and Manuel Monterrey. *Americanos: Latino Life in the United States*. New York: Little, Brown and Co., 1999.

Internet Resources

http://nacla.org

The North American Congress on Latin America provides information and news on Latin America. The group also analyzes what is going on in the region, especially as it relates to the United States.

http://lanic.utexas.edu/subject/countries.html

This directory offers links to dozens of informative websites, in Spanish and English, for each of the countries in Latin America and the Caribbean.

http://lcweb2.loc.gov/frd/cs/cshome.html#toc

Profiles of countries, including the Central American nations, with details about history, culture, and economics. Though some profiles are a decade out of date, they offer excellent background information.

http://www.pewhispanic.org

The Pew Hispanic Center provides analysis and reports on issues affecting Hispanics in the United States. The site is a trove of information for immigration, both legal and illegal.

http://www.uscis.gov/graphics/index.htm

Home page for the U.S. Bureau of Citizenship and Immigration Services.

http://www.lulac.org

LULAC is the oldest Hispanic organization in the United States. Its home page provides useful information on the organization's programs as well as a comprehensive list of links to other sites.

Index

Numbers in ***bold italic*** refer to captions.

Contributors

Senior consulting editor STUART ANDERSON is an adjunct scholar at the Cato Institute and executive director of the National Foundation for American Policy. From August 2001 to January 2003, he served as executive associate commissioner for Policy and Planning and Counselor to the Commissioner at the Immigration and Naturalization Service. He spent four and a half years on Capitol Hill on the Senate Immigration Subcommittee, first for Senator Spencer Abraham and then as Staff Director of the subcommittee for Senator Sam Brownback. Prior to that, Stuart was Director of Trade and Immigration Studies at the Cato Institute, where he produced reports on the military contributions of immigrants and the role of immigrants in high technology. Stuart has published articles in the Wall Street Journal, New York Times, Los Angeles Times, and other publications. He has an M.A. from Georgetown University and a B.A. in Political Science from Drew University. His articles have appeared in such publications as the *Wall Street Journal*, *New York Times*, and *Los Angeles Times*.

MARIAN L. SMITH served as the senior historian of the U.S. Immigration and Naturalization Service (INS) from 1988 to 2003, and is currently the immigration and naturalization historian within the Department of Homeland Security in Washington, D.C. She studies, publishes, and speaks on the history of the immigration agency and is active in the management of official 20th-century immigration records.

PETER HAMMERSCHMIDT is director general of national cyber security at Public Safety Canada. He previously served as First Secretary (Financial and Military Affairs) for the Permanent Mission of Canada to the United Nations. Before taking this position, he was a ministerial speechwriter and policy specialist for the Department of National Defence in Ottawa. Prior to joining the public service, he served as the Publications Director for the Canadian Institute of Strategic Studies in Toronto. He has a B.A. (Honours) in Political Studies from Queen's University, and an MScEcon in Strategic Studies from the University of Wales, Aberystwyth.

LUIS MARTINEZ is a freelance writer and editor. He was born in New Jersey and graduated from Yale. He is an award-winning daily newspaper journalist who has worked in New Jersey and Arizona, where he now lives with his wife and two children.

Picture Credits